D1231651

HARVARD POLITICAL STUDIES
PUBLISHED UNDER THE DIRECTION OF THE
DEPARTMENT OF GOVERNMENT IN
HARVARD UNIVERSITY

Harvard Political Studies

American Conservatism

IN THE AGE OF ENTERPRISE

American Conservatism

IN THE AGE OF ENTERPRISE

A STUDY OF WILLIAM GRAHAM SUMNER
STEPHEN J. FIELD AND ANDREW CARNEGIE

Robert Green McCloskey

HARVARD UNIVERSITY PRESS · CAMBRIDGE · MASSACHUSETTS
1951

TO MY MOTHER

FOREWORD

This volume is concerned with the evolution of conservative political thought in a crucial period of American intellectual history, extending roughly from the close of the Civil War through the first decade of the twentieth century. More specifically, it is focused on the rationale that was created in that era to justify the exemption of business enterprise from unwanted government interference. This body of ideas — "laissez faire" is the popular though imprecise term — reached full flower in America during those years and was, I believe, the dominant strain in the contemporary political mentality. It is my thesis that this conservative triumph was facilitated by a degeneration in the liberal democratic tradition, and the main purpose of this study is to examine the nature of that development.

To that end, I have chosen to consider three representative thinkers of the post-bellum period and have tried to illustrate how the transfiguration of American ideals is reflected in the social theories they espoused. Also — since one of these men was an academician, another a jurist, and the third a "captain of industry" — I have attempted to suggest how each of these areas of American life was related to the general movement of thought in the age of enterprise. The end product of this inquiry will be, I hope, a somewhat clearer understanding of a significant phase in the shaping of the American mind.

A word should perhaps be said about the use of terms. "Conservatism" and "liberalism" are words that can raise nice definitional problems, but from the viewpoint of these essays the problems are more intriguing than they are important, and I have used "conservatism" more as an identification than as a description. The doctrines considered here are organically related to earlier thinking that has been conventionally regarded as conservative, and the convention seems accurate enough to justify me in following it.

No effort has been made here to document the survival of these nineteenth-century postulates in present-day America. But that they do survive goes almost without saying. Some years have passed since a President of the United States declared that "the business of America is business." The epigram would surely be accepted less warmly today. Yet the tradition he spoke for still haunts the framers of public policy, still echoes in the dicta of publicists and statesmen, still rouses vibrations in the public mind. Modern proponents of these doctrines are more sophisticated perhaps than some of their predecessors, but the core of the argument is little altered. It rests on that inversion in liberal principles which is our nineteenth-century heritage.

It is both difficult and pleasant to acknowledge the part played by teachers, friends, and colleagues in making this book possible. The difficulty arises, of course, from the realization that the debts are too many and varied to be acknowledged in full. But the pleasure of mentioning a few such obligations is nonetheless great. Among my colleagues at Harvard, I am especially thankful to Professor Merle Fainsod, who made the original suggestion out of which this enterprise grew; to Professor Louis Hartz, whose acumen and knowledge have helped to enlarge my understanding of many things, including the subject matter of these studies; and to Professor William Yandell Elliott, who will, I hope, find reflected here a viewpoint concerning the nature of democracy which is recognizably and understandably akin to his own. Thanks are due to Miss Alice Green, who aided in the preparation of the manuscript. Professor Francis W. Coker of Yale University read the manuscript, and his scholarly criticism and advice have been helpful to me in a very real sense. The heaviest obligation of all is to President Benjamin F. Wright of Smith College, from whom I learned much of what I may know about American political thought and constitutional history, who steered the manuscript through its original draftings, and whose help and friendship have been invaluable throughout.

Most of the material of Chapter One, in a somewhat different form, appeared as an article in *The Review of Politics*, vol. XIII, no. 1 (January 1951), and is included here with the permission of the editors of that journal.

R. G. McC.

Cambridge, Massachusetts
August 1951

CONTENTS

one

CONSERVATISM AND DEMOCRACY

I

In 1873, an Associate Justice of the United States Supreme Court filed a memorable dissenting opinion. His brethren had upheld a state-granted monopoly against the charge that it violated the new Fourteenth Amendment. The substance of that majority judgment in the *Slaughter-House Cases* has never been reversed, and it stands today as a great milestone in our constitutional law.[1] But the dissent of Mr. Justice Field, though unproductive concerning the specific constitutional doctrine he there espoused, is, from another viewpoint, even more noteworthy. For it marks — or we can conveniently take it as marking — the point in our intellectual history at which the democratic strain in the American tradition begins its subservience to political conservatism.

The choice of a date is indeed somewhat arbitrary. A profound change in the national consciousness does not occur overnight, and the revision of the American ideology that Field's dissent proclaimed was not yet complete in 1873. But Field was a child of his times, and he spoke with the voice of the new generation. His rambling discourse, with its moral overtones, was evidence that a new era in American political thinking had dawned.

To understand the nature of the change that was given

documentation in this dissent, it is necessary to explore briefly some of the wellsprings of American democratic ideals. And here, it must be confessed at the outset, generalizations are perilous. American democracy in its inception rested on such a diverse array of abstract doctrines, semireligious convictions, and economic motivations that it is venturesome to make dogmatic assertions about its fundamental character. Lacking an authoritative messiah, such as Marxism for example enjoys, the interpreter of democratic political thought is forced to acknowledge exceptions to any generality he propounds. He is compelled to seek what he believes to be the emphasis, rather than the clearly delineated path, of the democratic tradition; he follows, not a well-marked road, but a "tendency."

Yet consideration of one such tendency in early American thinking is essential to an understanding of what took place in the minds of the post-Civil War generation. The language Field used in his dissent was reminiscent of the radical democrats of the revolutionary era; some of his phrases were, in fact, lifted bodily from the Declaration of Independence. But the meaning now attached to those words was peculiarly Fieldian, wrenched to harmonize with a different concept of liberty and justice. For, with the cautions already noted, it seems correct to say that the Jeffersonian theory of democracy was rooted in spiritual and humane, rather than material and economic, values. That is, when the revolutionary democrat spoke of equality, he was concerned primarily with an essential equality of men before God, a sharing by all in the same basic humanness. Such a concept is obviously more closely related to the Stoic tradition in Western thought than to Justice Field's notion of equality in the right "to choose a vocation." Again, when he used the term "liberty," the early democrat meant, first of all, freedom of conscience — moral liberty — rather than freedom of business enterprise. His chief interest, in short, was in the right of the individual to realize his moral personality, and not the right to buy and sell and prosper economically. Justice Field, on the other hand, was patently using these root democratic catchwords and ideals in a quite different frame of reference. For him and for generations of his countrymen who followed, economic liberty and democratic liberty were inextricably associated; and the democratic tradition as they understood it thus presented an almost insuperable obstacle to programs of economic reform.

There are several reasons why these misapprehensions developed and why they persisted in post-bellum America. For one thing, there was, and to a large extent still is, a failure to recognize that in democracy, as in other moral systems, different levels of value can be distinguished. The true and central concern of American democracy is the morally free individual; the right of this individual to maintain his dignity and develop his moral capacities is at the apex of the democratic value hierarchy. But the recognition of this end value as primary involves the acknowledgment of certain subvalues which are always indispensable to its realization. For example, moral liberty cannot flourish if freedom of speech is denied, nor can it survive in a community without religious toleration. Hence freedom of speech and religion must be regarded as democratically basic, not, however, because they are ends in themselves, but because they are essential to the attainment of democracy's primary ideals. And finally, at a still lower level in the democratic hierarchy may be found such other instrumental values as economic freedom, whose claim to binding validity is contingent, dependent, on shifting external circumstances. Values in this category are not indeed irrelevant to the democratic tradition, since there may be times when economic restraints would inhibit moral self-development. But these values are not basic; they are not self-justifying; they stand in relation to the democratic primary values as means to ends.

Now some such value hierarchy as this is clearly implicit in the body of doctrines that were summarized in the opening sentences of the Declaration of Independence. For the American democrat of Jefferson's model, humane or moral freedom occupied the higher place, while economic freedom was subordinate. And I have suggested that one reason this is not always clear is because the observer fails to recognize that there are such distinctions, or at any rate fails to apply them to the historical analysis. It must be conceded, however, that another reason for misunderstanding is a certain ambiguity in the sources themselves. It is a fact — and an important one — that early democratic theory in America was never systematically worked out, so that one will search in vain in the writings of contemporary spokesmen for a consistent statement of the hierarchy of ideals that has been proposed. In the polemics before and during the Revolution, the right to "the means of acquiring and possessing property" was often treated as if it were fundamental, and we only occasionally find evidence that any distinction was drawn between one kind of democratic right and another.

Some understanding of this ambiguity and the reasons for it therefore becomes important. The democratic theory which the American Revolution inherited was first expressed in seventeenth-century England by the Puritans of the left. It was they who expounded the political ideals that later became typical of radical democracy. Now in the thinking of these dissenters, the emphasis is clearly on the side of spiritual or humane values; the instrumental and secondary character of the property right is assumed. "The poorest he that is in England hath a life to live as the richest he" means simply that the right of the individual to live a full life is superior to any contradictory claims resting on the possession of property. Social action should primarily aim to create conditions that will make it possible to realize what A. D. Lindsay has called "the fundamental Christian doctrine of the absolute worth of the individual soul." To forward this end, the radicals pressed for economic and political concessions which, if granted, would have changed the whole fabric of English society. In the case of the Levellers, the demand was made for a share in political rule; the Diggers spoke out for communal sharing of property. But for both factions, the central ideal was not these measures themselves, but the new moral life for the common man which their realization would open up. Both groups were concerned in the first instance, not with institutional forms, but with humanity.

This Christian democratic tradition was to some degree implicit in the inheritance Locke drew on when he set out to justify the Glorious Revolution, but it was already overlaid by another, more materialist, credo. As Laski has said, there were in the English seventeenth century two revolutions, the one represented by Winstanley and Lilburne, the other by Cromwell and Ireton. Similarly, democratic thought received two infusions, the first from the radical Christian democrats already mentioned, the second from the sober-sided English middle class, bent on shaping a doctrine congenial to men of property. And with Locke this second element in the nascent democratic tradition was reformulated and reinforced, for Locke was a thinker very different from the Puritan radicals. In his hands, at least in the *Second Treatise*, the right of private property became in effect an end in itself, became indeed the typical right, the analogy on which the argument for all other rights was based. It would be hard to contend that for Locke the protection of property was merely instrumental to the maintenance of a more fundamental ideal. There is, it is true, some basis for doubting that Locke claimed the status of natural right for all types of property however acquired. It has been argued that, for Locke, man has a natural right only to that property with which he has mixed his labor and which he can personally use;[2] it may well be that some such distinction lurks behind the curious obscurities of the *Second Treatise*. But whatever his intention may have been, Locke's expression of it was ambiguous; and the practical effect of his thought was undoubtedly to justify not only the Glorious Revolution but Western capitalism. So, whether intentionally or not, Locke fastened on democracy the idea that the right of private property is fundamental; he set in train a materialization of democratic ideals that led ultimately to their perversion.

Thus two variant and potentially contradictory democratic traditions move together through the intellectual turmoils of the eighteenth century, to be taken up and used, when the time comes, by the apologists for the American Revolution. The one is primarily a humane doctrine, emphasizing the worth of the individual, and assigning the rights of private property to a subordinate, instrumental position; the other is not indifferent to these humane values, to be sure, but it elevates the property right to the same plane and thus saddles democratic theory with a paradox. It is a paradox, however, whose existence often goes unobserved, and there are hard practical reasons why this is so. The effective appeal of abstractions is always greater when they can be associated with some concrete interest: a loss of property is more tangible and evident than a loss of moral freedom and is more apt therefore, in this imperfect world, to stir men's swift indignation. Democratic forces found powerful and indispensable support in the rising bourgeois class; and if the ultimate effects of the alliance were pernicious — as I contend — the immediate effect was to stimulate the growth of democratic institutions. By the time American revolutionary thinkers began to formulate their ideas, the property right was firmly established as an article of the democratic creed, and its prestige was enhanced by the circumstance that the British "tyranny" threatened the economic interests of many colonists. So, while a democratic thinker might have believed that human rights are superior to the rights of property, he rarely made the distinction explicit, partly because his premises were not clearly thought out, and partly because the support of property-conscious colonists was essential to the success of the democratic revolutionary program.

The democratic arguments of the revolutionary period present us then with an unclarified ideological pattern, and we can hardly blame a later generation for assuming that all the conventional revolutionary values carried equal weights. History is indeed "a pack of tricks we play on the dead," and each era reads the thought of the last in the shadow of its own presuppositions. The post-Civil War generation, biased in favor of economic freedom to an almost obsessive degree, could not perhaps be expected to look beyond the bare words of the revolutionists to discover an "emphasis" on the less tangible, humane values of democracy. Field found in the revolutionary tradition what he wanted to find and troubled himself with no subtleties.

Yet an appreciation of this emphasis, a recognition of these subtleties, is necessary to an understanding of the revolutionary period and essential to a comparison of that era with what Mark Twain called the "Gilded Age." For, in spite of Ireton and Locke, in spite of the economic motivations of the colonial merchants, democratic theory in the revolutionary period was still a humane philosophy; the process of corrosion that began in the seventeenth century had not yet completely subverted the democratic faith.

The basic value judgments of liberal democratic theory were, as has been suggested, a secular reformulation of Christian normative premises. These judgments, though secularized by 1776, had not yet lost their original character. That character had only been obscured somewhat by an overlay of purely bourgeois ideology. When Jefferson essayed a summary of liberal theory in the stately opening sentences of the Declaration, he gave testimony to the survival of the root democratic values. To quote Carl Becker:

It [the natural rights philosophy of the Declaration] furnished at once a justification and a profound emotional inspiration for the revolutionary movements of the seventeenth and eighteenth centuries. Founded upon a superficial knowledge of history it was, certainly; and upon a naïve faith in the instinctive virtues of human kind. Yet it was a humane and engaging faith. At its best it preached toleration in place of persecution, goodwill in place of hate, peace in place of war. It taught that beneath all local and temporary diversity, beneath the superficial traits and talents that distinguish men and nations, all men are equal in the possession of a common humanity; and to the end that concord might prevail on the earth instead of strife, it invited men to promote in themselves the humanity which bound them to their fellows, and to shape their conduct and their institutions in harmony with it.[3]

It would almost seem that no one could read this statement, or for that matter the affirmations of the Declaration itself, and retain the idea that in this philosophy property occupied as exalted a place as humanity. But the literal-minded have always been ill at ease with these democratic abstractions. For the populist leader, William Jennings Bryan, equality "in the possession of a common humanity" was interpreted to mean that every man in Tennessee had an equal claim to judge the validity of the Darwinian hypothesis.[4] For American philistines from 1776 onward, and with increasing consistency, "liberty" was translated as the freedom to engage in economic enterprise, while the more basic and humane significance of the term was gradually submerged. And by 1873, when Field invoked the Declaration of Independence in his defense of property rights, the democratic credo was no longer recognizable; it had been, like Hegel's dialectic, turned upside down.

What had happened in the meantime? How was it that the ideals of democracy could be so cavalierly used? And why was it, above all, that so little counterargument was directed at the heart of Field's thesis — the assumption that the philosophy of the Declaration was mainly focused on material, economic values? Part of the answer to these queries has already been suggested. Field's generalizations and others like them went essentially unchallenged because, for one thing, the democratic faith had never been converted into a logically consistent ideology and, for another, because the documents of that faith lent a certain specious support to these interpretations. But though these circumstances are important, they are not conclusive. For a fuller explanation it is necessary to go deeper and penetrate the social context out of which Field wrote. Then we can see that his gloss on the Declaration was uncontested largely because it expressed the tacit convictions of most of his fellows. They too had transvalued the values of democracy; they too had learned to read the old symbols of the American faith by a new light; they too looked back on the revolutionary movement and saw it principally as a crusade to secure the rights of property. And the force that played on men's minds and made them receptive to this perversion of democratic ideals found its source in the contemporary industrial order. The striking fact in postbellum political thought is that the rise of industrial capitalism in America transfigured the going concept of democracy as it had transfigured so many other elements in the social fabric. Even before Field wrote, Marx and Engels had analyzed the development he illustrates:

The bourgeoisie, wherever it has got the upper hand, has put an end to all feudal, patriarchal, idyllic relations. It has pitilessly torn asunder the motley feudal ties that bound man to his "natural superiors," and has left no other nexus between man and man than naked self-interest, than callous "cash payment." It has drowned the most heavenly ecstacies of religious fervour, of chivalrous enthusiasm, of philistine sentimentalism, in the icy water of egotistical calculation. It has resolved personal worth into exchange value, and in place of the numberless, indefeasible chartered freedoms, has set up that single unconscionable freedom — Free Trade.[5]

Now this shift in the character of American norms, this resolving of "personal worth into exchange value," did not begin with the nineteenth century. The tendency toward the new habit of mind set in long before, when feudal ties began to be strained under pressure from the new commercial class. But the headlong advance of American capitalism in the 1800's, and particularly after Appomattox, greatly accelerated the trend; the natural human inclination to materialize abstractions was increasingly abetted by a social and industrial order in which abstractions seemed to have no meaning.

Neither must capitalism stand indicted alone as the proximate cause of this evolution in society's value structure. Contributing factors played their part. Scientific advance seemed on the point of dispelling life's mysteries, and a strong impression prevailed that, though there might be unknowns, the Unknowable was a false conception. And since the knowable was, by hypothesis, the measurable, the reduction of all human standards to matter-of-fact terms seemed imminent. Darwin and Spencer had opened up shining new vistas of scientism.[6] The steady urbanization attendant on industrial growth similarly eroded the "sentimental" bases of social relationships. Crowded together in apartment houses and slums, men lost touch with the value world they had formerly inhabited; the subordination of "every human quality in design to 'amount of value considered quantitatively' " degraded the national ideals.[7] When John Bright, to Arnold's disgust, equated the greatness and goodness of Britain with the size of her cities and the vastness of her industrial resources, he was but echoing a refrain that had come to be taken for granted by the urban Briton or American.

However we may choose to answer the riddle of causation (and much more could be said on this point), there is abundant evidence of the fact itself — that American thought patterns had been invaded by a profoundly materialist bias. By a kind of ironic paradox, this development is nowhere better illustrated than by the new Christianity that bloomed in the industrial age. Fundamentalist preachers, confronted by the explanations science advanced for the origin of the species, could find no answer but the doctrine of literal biblical interpretation. It seems not to have occurred to them to exploit the real strength of religion in the nonmaterial realm of spiritual truth; instead, they impeached their cause by disputing with science in its own empirical terms. As further evidence of their submission to a materialist standard, the idea of natural law, which had bulked so large in the American heritage, was perverted by these divines into a religious sanction of the industrial order: Godliness was said to be "in league with riches."[8] In 1891, Rudyard Kipling listened to a man of God who epitomized the trend:

With a voice of silver and with imagery borrowed from the auction-room, he built up for his hearers a heaven on the lines of the Palmer House (but with all the gilding real gold and all the plate-glass diamond) and set in the center of it a loud-voiced, argumentative, and very shrewd creation that he called God. One sentence at this point caught my delighted ear. It was apropos of some question of the Judgment, and ran: "No! I tell you God doesn't do business that way."[9]

Thus God and the worship of Him in the new industrial Atlantis. Meanwhile, inevitably, the debasement of values was extending into other fields. The going concept of human worth underwent a certain metamorphosis. The "feudal ties that bound man to his 'natural superiors'" were indeed worn away, but to be replaced by a new concept of elitism, a new order of merit — the fraternity of wealth. Election to the ranks of this parvenu aristocracy was, in Veblen's terms, on the basis of "pecuniary aptitudes"; the standard of worthiness became business success. A kind of mystic veneration was accorded to the man who could "buy and sell" his less competent contemporaries. As the age wore on, this deference toward the captain of industry was supplied with a rationale; his leadership and privilege were justified on the pretext that he was society's benefactor.[10] But this was *post facto* reasoning. In the beginning, the canonization of the man of substance was purely instinctive, a tacit acknowledgment of the new materialist faith.

A like spirit can be detected in the idea of progress that captured the imagination of the Gilded Age. Classical economics and the concept of organic evolution conspired to change the old doctrine of the moral improvement of man into a theory of material progress.[11] In general, prophets of the nineteenth century clung to that notion of a beneficent natural order which had so intoxicated the philosophers in the age of reason. But how different were the modern natural laws, drained of all ethical content, and how different was the millennium now envisioned as the capstone of progress! Civilization was equated with industrialization, and progress was defined as the accumulation of capital and the proliferation of industrial inventions.[12]

The effect of all this on artistic and literary taste has been too often noted and documented to need much reiteration. The "success novel" was only the most obvious manifestation of aesthetic and moral deterioration. Architecture was cheapened almost everywhere. Great, hideous mansions were built by a whole drove of Silas Laphams. Within, they were stuffed with heavy, grotesque furniture whose only justification for existence was its palpable cost. The standard of taste in public construction was, if anything, worse than in private building; with the outstanding exception of Richardson, "cheap jerry builders and ignorant engineers" were considered good enough to design the post offices and churches that so tellingly reflect the *Zeitgeist* of a community.[13]

II

It would have been strange indeed if this general deterioration of standards and ideals had not been reflected in the political thought of the era, if it had not altered in some substantial respects the presumptions of American democracy. Surely a combination of circumstances that brought about the most radical transformation of all other mores could not have left the political folk beliefs of the nation untouched. Yet it is curious how few discussions of American political thought recognize a shift at this point in the character of political norms. There is no dearth of studies recording the hegemony of business in the political decisions of the era; nor, on the other hand, is there any failure to recognize that, in the late nineteenth century, American life and thought were permeated with the gospel of wealth. But the relationship between these two egregious facts is only dimly seen. The existence of a corrupt alliance between business and politics was not discovered by Lincoln Steffens. Years before *The Shame of the Cities* swam into the ken of American readers, its general premises were commonplace.[14] The cause for wonder is not that the businessmen and politicians of the era struck a dirty bargain, but that the contract was permitted to endure. The remarkable thing is not that business tended to fatten and develop monopolistic traits and to exercise an autocratic control over the lives and destinies of Americans.

The extraordinary fact is that, in a technically free land, industry was allowed to indulge those propensies subject to no effective restraint by the body politic.

The enigma is not explained by the suggestion that the political leaders of the people were the hirelings of the business community. Insofar as this is true, it is only the outer shell of an explanation, for it fails to account for the acquiescence of the voters in this shabby arrangement. More important, it neglects to explain those numerous instances of governmental subservience to business in which a naïve bargain could hardly have played a part — the decisions of the Supreme Court for one notable example.

Nor is it tenable to blame democracy as Henry Adams seemed to do, to take refuge in the generality that the people are easily hoodwinked and basically unfit to rule themselves. Democracy is a norm as well as a plan of government, and when the one decays the other must share the contamination. It was not democracy but a perversion of it which was used to justify the excesses of capital in the post-bellum era, and the perversion, not the doctrine, should be blamed. Adams' Senator Radcliffe was not the inevitable product of an application of democratic ideals: he *was* the inevitable product of the misapplication of those ideals, a misunderstanding of democracy's central message, and a degradation of its faith.

Most students of American political thought have assumed that the national attitude toward such ideals as liberty and individualism has been relatively constant. Especially they have assumed that these terms have always been wedded to a concept of economic "laissez faire" in political philosophy and in the popular understanding.[15] The postwar resistance to governmental regulation of business is seen then as merely the continuation of a traditional democratic bias. But the truth is that no such continuity exists. The democratic ideals to which Field paid his respects were radically different and logically incompatible with the humane philosophy of the Declaration whose terminology he borrowed. But by taking advantage of an initial ambiguity, by exploiting the vast prestige which the businessman had acquired, Field, William Graham Sumner, Andrew Carnegie, Bishop Lawrence, and other lay and clerical apostles of the gospel of wealth were able to weld capitalism to the democratic creed. They were able thereby to capture democracy and make it hostage to conservatism, so that the aims of democracy and those of business became indistinguishable in the popular view.

What has befallen American democratic thought in this transition is simply told. In the first place, economic freedom, which is, properly speaking, a means, a subsidiary value in the democratic hierarchy, has assumed the status of an end in itself. It is easy to say that this involves only a shift in emphasis, but the shift becomes profoundly important when we recognize that it throws the scales into a new balance. The idea of a free economic system now stands on an equal plane with the concept of moral liberty. Secondly, this equal position of economic values in the democratic hierarchy is changed to one of preponderance. That is, the spokesmen of the new cause, having established the proposition that economic freedom is *a* primary value, are in a position to give the impression by judicious emphasis that it is *the* primary value. This is possible partly because of the logical impracticability of serving two conflicting ideal ends; partly because people's minds have been prepared for this intellectual conquest by the corrosion of standards in other realms; and partly because the instruments for molding public opinion are in the hands of those who have most to gain by an acceptance of the new dogmas.

Hence not only a new concept of democracy but a new conservative rationale develops on the moribund body of Jeffersonian liberalism. It is important to the effectiveness of

this latter-day gospel that, although a different political value
system had gained currency, the people as a whole were unaware of the fact. The conservatives of an earlier period —
Ames, Hamilton, Kent, Morris, Marshall, and the rest — had
wasted little love on democracy. In general, the Hamiltonians
reluctantly conceded the necessity of some popular participation in political decisions, and then devoted themselves to
minimizing the effects of the concession as much as possible.
Except in such publications as the *Federalist*, where an out-
right rejection of republican principles would have defeated
the purpose, Hamilton himself hardly bothered to hide his
hostility to the premises of popular government. But with the
extension of the franchise and the popular movements of the
Jacksonian period, it became obvious that the ideology of
democracy was irresistible. It was no longer practical for
public figures to reject the Jeffersonian precepts openly;
those precepts had become universally accepted and could
no more be foresworn than could the axioms of the Sermon
on the Mount.

Lip service to the catchwords of democracy, then, was
inescapable. But there was, on the other hand, nothing to
prevent a modification of their meanings, provided the change
was subtle enough to escape general observation. And that
is of course exactly what took place: the traditional terms
were drained of their old significance; a new content was in-
jected; and it was generally supposed that nothing had happened, because the labels remained unchanged. The conservative exponent of a basically antidemocratic ethos could
now bolster up his argument with the language of democracy
itself.

I am not suggesting, of course, that the prophets of this
new conservatism carried out a deliberate fraud, that they
saw the problem as it has just been stated and realized that
the way to defeat the partisans of democracy was to join

them. It is doubtful if an important modification in popular doctrine has ever been engineered in such a fashion, and certainly nothing of the sort happened here. What gave Field's arguments such a righteous ring and made them so compelling was his own acceptance of them, his patent conviction that the moral law was on his side. Throughout the period, indeed, the presumption of immorality rested on those who would detract from the rewards of capital. There was no indecency in depriving the new freedmen of protection for their civil rights by a subtle and strained interpretation of the Fourteenth Amendment.[16] But a reading of the direct tax clause of the Constitution backed by historical evidence and a century of precedent was viewed with horror, because it sanctioned a federal income tax.[17] We can accept the sincerity of the railroad tycoon who felt national honor was besmirched by a law that required the roads to pay their bonded indebtedness.[18] He was merely expressing, albeit in somewhat extreme form, the going standard of success-morality. The proponents of a capitalistic ethic all adopted the same tone and found a ready audience, because the fundamental premises of that audience were identical with their own. In a value system that acknowledges only material ideals, the property right obviously enjoys a special sanctity. Field simply made articulate a conclusion that had become logically unescapable; and he spoke not as a prophet from a strange land, but as the authentic voice of nineteenth-century America.

Nor is it pretended that conversion to the new faith took place all at once or that the break in continuity was sharp and clear. The conflict in democratic theory between the rights of property and the rights of man began at least as early as 1642 and was never explicitly resolved. Throughout the eighteenth and early nineteenth centuries, under the influence of growing industrialization, the prestige of property-rights democracy gradually increased, but the concept of human rights, though attenuating, remained predominant. By 1870, however, the pressure of the capitalist ethic can no longer be denied; its claim to dominance in the national tradition is firmly established; and the 1870's mark therefore a turning point in American democratic thinking. The gospel of wealth is not unfamiliar before that time, nor is the voice of the genuine democratic creed completely silenced thereafter. But the relationship between them has been altered; the new era of conservatism has begun.

In this new reading, democracy is no longer a progressive faith. Or, more accurately, what passes for the democratic dogma becomes as serviceable to conservatism as to liberalism. And since the advantage in an ideological stalemate lies with the side favoring the *status quo*, conservatism reaps a net gain. Henceforward the American people are guided by a devitalized political philosophy; faced with an issue for political decision, they are torn between contradictory impulses. On the one hand, they sense the need to regulate economic enterprise in the interests of society as a whole. On the other hand, they feel morally bound to cleave to the principle of "laissez faire." The result is that the popular will is immobilized; it fails to act, or acts only with hesitation. The confusion of thought that John Locke imposed on the democratic ideology has become an impasse.

An analysis of this impasse is helpful to an understanding of American political behavior during the past century. The identification of democracy with the property right gave rise to an ambivalent national attitude toward problems of social reform. Since most positive social programs in an industrial age necessarily involve some curtailment of economic freedom, the advocate of such programs finds himself at odds with an accepted postulate of democracy. The citizen who feels that something should be done to mitigate the power of

industrial combinations over the lives and destinies of individuals is at the same time troubled by the suspicion that
such a restraint on industry would outrage the democratic
faith. His natural concern for social amelioration cannot be
altogether suppressed; but it can be prevented from taking
the shape of positive governmental action, because it is at
this point that the logical conflict in democratic objectives
will arise. The sympathetic impulses of America find expression only in a great flowering of "anti-cruelty" movements
and limited-objective private charities. A relatively light
checkrein on political movements toward a similar end is suf-
ficient to curb the forces of economic reform.

It has often been observed, for example, that the persistence and general acceptance of judicial review reflects a conservative strain in the American political character. There
can be no doubts that the Supreme Court was, from the 1870's
on, a citadel of American conservatism. But the success of
the courts in defending a conservative doctrine must be explained in the light of the paradox that the American political temperament is not only conservative but humane and
liberal as well. We must account for the fact that Americans,
having voted for and set in motion programs of economic
reform, have so often been acquiescent when those programs
were frustrated by judicial veto. Part of the answer can be
found, I think, in the proposition that the legislative program
and the veto of the Court represent two sides of the American
political personality, each of which finds its roots in an interpretation of democratic ideals. The citizen who votes for a
progressive measure is dimly aware that in doing so he denies
one absolute value while attempting to carry out the implications of another. Starting with such incoherently divided
loyalties, his will to see his mandate realized is hesitant to
begin with; and the rejection of the measure by the judiciary
is accepted, not only because it relieves him of further obli-

gation to puzzle over his own irreconcilable premises, but
also because the Court's view is in a sense his own, like the
"Real Will" in Bosanquet's theory.

III

Thus the nature of the conservative ideology that developed in the latter half of the nineteenth century begins to
be clear. It does not take the form of a sharply distinguishable
doctrine counterpoised against the progressive democratic
tradition, as in the earlier period. No longer is it practical —
or necessary — to inveigh against the shibboleths of democracy. It is far more convenient to make use of the reverence
attached to democratic symbols, to harness the horsepower
of democracy to the conservative cart. Thereafter conservatism, far from standing in opposition to democracy, takes its
place as an integral part of the democratic value system. Conservatism, to paraphrase a well-worn Communist Party slo-
gan, becomes nineteenth-century Americanism.

This marriage of conservatism to democracy was made
possible, as we have seen, by a materialization of community
value standards, which was in turn largely induced by the
impact of industrial capitalism on American society. It is interesting to observe in this connection that both Veblen and
Parrington have not merely missed this point, but have stood
it on its head. In Veblen, the assumption is made throughout
that the resilience of conservative dogmas depends on society's *failure* to adopt a materialist, matter-of-fact habit of
mind.[19] And by implication at least, though Veblen is always
obscure on such points, the suggestion is made that the political progressiveness of a society will be in direct ratio to its
acceptance of materialist rather than "archaic" extra-material
value standards. In Parrington, the inference is drawn even
more clearly. He sees "critical realism" as a healthy breeze
blowing away the conservative miasmas of the past and

bringing with it a point of view that seems to him, genially liberal as he is, almost wholly beneficent. "To get back once more on the main-travelled road, to put away all profitless romanticisms and turn realist" [20] — these were the objectives of his progressivism; and we are led to believe that the liberal democratic tradition succeeds or fails as it adopts those guides. He ignores the robust conservative doctrine compounded of Spencerian Darwinism, Malthusianism, and classical economics that was erected on just such a groundwork. He blinks the fact that, while materialism did of course produce social critics, it disarmed them for the very encounter they essayed and produced to oppose them a new and colder brand of conservatism. Democratic liberalism did not, to be sure, even in the nineteenth century, entirely surrender to the capitalist ideology, and the history of the period is in part one of struggle against the dominance of the gospel of wealth. But the current of social criticism is weakened by the circumstance that the conservative forces have laid claim to democracy, and it is further weakened by the failure of most dissenters to recognize this fact and explore its implications. Had they done so, I suggest that they might have traced the conservative argument back to its roots in a postwar confusion of democratic premises, and that they would have then been in position to resolve the confusion and set the liberal faith back on the path whence it had strayed.

two

THE WORLD OF WILLIAM GRAHAM SUMNER

I

Such terms as "conservatism" and "liberalism" lend themselves easily to semantic confusion, but this is not to say that they have no meaning. In American political thought they are convenient shorthand for describing a fairly consistent cleavage in basic doctrines. The native conservative has traditionally identified himself with certain root postulates about the ideal political order and has cast about him in each new era for telling arguments to support these articles of faith. But though the argumentative façade may tend to obscure, it cannot conceal the underlying structure: in each era the aims of conservatism have been much the same.

In general, its advocates have defended the property right against all comers, exalting economic privilege to the status of an absolute. This is perhaps the leitmotiv, but other recurrent strains can be distinguished. In the same chorus we are almost certain to find those who deplore the rule of the majority in political decision-making. At first, this opposition to popular rule is frank and explicit and takes the form of legal restrictions of the suffrage.[1] Later, when manhood suffrage has been generally established, the opposition becomes more usually an appeal to constitutionalism, an invocation of the limits on popular rule implied by the original social compact. Finally, in this category are ordinarily discovered those who espouse an elitist doctrine, a concept of the natural superiority of the few — which is used, of course, to justify the defense of privilege and the limitation of the majority will.

Historically, the partisans of such a set of attitudes have occupied a defensive position in the American political scene. The *status quo* has supported their claims, and deviations from the *status quo* have therefore called those claims into question. The defenders have, in the nature of things, based their case partly on an appeal to the past and partly on a glorification of the golden present. Thus it is pragmatically valid to call them conservatives, though it is important to observe that the really significant distinguishing characteristic is not the "conserving" element but adherence to the dogmas just outlined.

But if certain premises have been more or less consistently held by conservatives in American history, there have been significant variations in their less fundamental professions and beliefs. And it is these variations that have given rise to the easy generalization that the term "conservatism" is itself meaningless. For a political faith must offer not only a statement of basic aims but a program of action — or inaction — and a rationale. Yet neither the program nor the justification can be static for long; each must be altered from time to time as objective circumstances change, raising new problems both of method and ideology.

With respect to program, the most obvious example of such alteration is to be found in the shifting conservative attitude toward government intervention in business affairs. Hamilton, of course, had proposed the active coöperation of business and government for the greater glory of both the commonwealth and the propertied interests; [2] and this Hamiltonian ideal, while never unanimously approved, was an element in conservative doctrine throughout the first seventy-five years of the Republic. After the Civil War, however, it became clear that capitalism was now strong enough to get along without more active assistance from government than it already enjoyed. Equally important, it began to appear that in a partnership between government and business the danger of gratuitous political interference was becoming too serious to justify the risk.[3] The idea of a positive relationship between government and economic life thus fell out of favor among those who underwrote the conservative program.

But a mere statement of the case in these terms is enough to indicate that, in making this shift, conservatism had by no means departed from its main premises. The advantage of the propertied interests was the aim of both the Hamiltonian and the post-bellum programs, and the difference was only in the choice of means. The change had been impelled partly by a broadening of government's popular base, which aggravated the threat of encroaching legislation, and partly by an unexampled increase in the independent vitality of the business community.

Such a shift in the externals of the doctrine is characteristic of the history of American conservatism. The deeper-lying principles — property rights, antipopulism, and elitism — have been constant, but the nature of the political measures these concepts implied has varied in conformity with a changing historical context. So too with the character of the rationale conservatism employed to support its central dogmas: the history has been one of retreat from successive intellectual strongholds. In Puritan days, the dogmas were sustained by religious sanctions, by a theology that culminated in a theory of the "elect." Later conservatives took refuge in an emphasis on secular class distinctions, a survival of the Old World culture pattern which attributed special merit and wisdom to the well-born.

But neither of these rationalizations was appropriate for the day that began to dawn in the nineteenth century. Privi-

lege based on an essentially feudal ideal of class prerogative
was harder and harder to maintain against the rising democratic spirit. More important perhaps, such a notion was at
odds with the facts of the new industrial civilization wherein
many a proud name came to grief and many a parvenu scaled
the heights. Nor was the Puritan ideal of a privileged elect
any more tenable as an explicit doctrine in the New World.
The concept survived as an inarticulate premise of conservative thought in the Gilded Age, but its sanctions were ultimately spiritual (though its implications were often mundane enough), and some more materialist rationale was
needed to suit the requirements of conservatism in the age of
science and industrial capitalism. By the 1870's the appeal to
a transcendental ethic and the appeal to a basically medieval
class tradition had lost much of their force. It was necessary
then to justify the rights of property in new terms, to find a
new rationalization for the inequality of power and privilege
which is implied in the root conservative credo, and to find
new spokesmen who could manipulate the unique postwar
idiom. And in the nature of things, this justification had to
rest, not alone on tradition or the will of God, but on utility;
these spokesmen had to be, not purveyors of an archaic ethical currency, but "realists" who conducted their transactions
in the hard coinage of objective fact.

For the materials of such a rejuvenated conservative rationale, the post-bellum generation had not far to seek. The
doctrines of classical economics had so far exerted a limited
influence over governmental policy in the United States, but
they had, in a diluted form, been transmitted to hosts of receptive students by way of such works as Francis Wayland's
Elements of Political Economy (1837) and Harriet Martineau's *Illustrations* (1832–1834).[4] Thus the economic case for
"laissez faire" stood ready to do service whenever the commercial world should require its good offices. It provided

conservative thinkers with a mythological construct called "the competitive order" in which "the pecuniary motive has its perfect work, and guides all the acts of economic man in a guileless, colorless, unswerving quest of the greatest gain at the least sacrifice." [5]

It is true that the postulates of academic political economy also implied an opposition to the protective tariff, an aspect of the creed that was not quite so salutary from the viewpoint of the captains of industry. But if the professors themselves were true to their principles and continued to advocate free trade, conservatism as a program for action and as a body of folk beliefs was under no such obligation to be consistent. Controlling the organs of communication, enjoying a degree of prestige that gave its utterances the stamp of infallibility, the rising generation of businessmen was able to select what it liked among the dogmas of the academicians and reject the remainder.

Even more important in helping to shape the argument for conservatism in the post-Appomattox world were the social and political analogies drawn from the biological insights of Charles Darwin.[6] In large part, of course, the findings of Darwin seemed to complement and confirm the hypotheses of the classical economists. Political economy taught that the maximum utility for society as a whole would be achieved if economic forces were allowed to work without restriction. Social Darwinism gave the ideal of noninterference enormously enhanced prestige by making it the *sine qua non* of all human progress. An unfettered industrial order would insure not only an optimum product in the world of today, but a perfect race and a perfect social order in the world of tomorrow. It was an engaging, even sometimes an inspiring, conception.

Even better, it was a conception made to the order of an industrial age. Its character, its terminology, its symbols were completely secular, purporting to rest on empirical truth, on concrete, scientific findings. No appeal need be taken to an abstract moral law for verification of the rules that govern a just society. One need only look to nature herself to trace the inexorable workings of those rules in the geologic record. Facts were what the postwar age understood best, and facts were what the Social Darwinists pretended to give it. Abstract ethics had lost much of its charm; very well, here was the basis for an ethic empirically derived. "This was a vast stride," said Henry Adams. "Unbroken evolution under uniform conditions pleased everyone — except curates and bishops; it was the very best substitute for religion; a safe, conservative, practical, thoroughly Common-Law deity." [7] And, although the philosophers who worked with these new materials — men like Spencer in England and Fiske in America [8] — often envisioned a flowering of individual personality at the rainbow's end, a "divine event" in Spencer's terms, what most men understood of Social Darwinism was its promise of constantly increasing material well-being. A system whose moral imperatives were dependent upon materialist proof, however, was doomed from the outset. The teleology of Fiske and the optimism of Spencer withered away in time from the main stalk, leaving only a cold determinism, a set of precepts devoid of moral content and glorifying selfishness in the name of science.

As the conservatives employed it, the Darwinian revelation supported all their traditional premises. In nature, the fittest rise to positions of dominance, the less fit are eliminated. Thus the species slowly improves through natural selection, so long as no extraneous influence interferes. At a blow then, the timeworn presumptions of American conservatism were given new confirmation. "Fitness" was defined in terms of material success, because nature is incapable of recognizing another standard. The elite, the saints of the new religion, therefore, were those who had proved their native superiority by their survival value. This will be recognized as the Puritan idea of "election" in modern dress; the supporting rationale was different, but the implications were almost indistinguishable. Inequality was no longer a dismal necessity as the economists had argued; it was a disguised blessing that helped move society onward and upward. The claim of the great body of the people to control the social order they live in was manifestly unwarranted. The inferiority of the masses was attested by their economic position, and the great social decisions must be left to those who had won the right to make them.

On similar grounds, the property right earned nature's sanction. Those most qualified to control property were those who had demonstrated their capacity in the competitive struggle. Movements to deprive them of control were ill advised in a double sense: first, because such action might disturb the cosmic plan and inhibit progress; but, second, because in some way not always clear, the acquisition of property somehow invested the owner with a moral right to hold his prize. This curious blending of an empirically derived moralism with deductions from the facts themselves was characteristic of the new commercial apologia. Pretending to reject abstract moral concepts, its exponents introduced one by the back door. The illusion of right and wrong is persistent and not dissipated by formal repudiation, and the prophets of the new faith owed more to the despised Enlightenment than they liked to acknowledge.

One might think, considering the aptness of these analogies, that Social Darwinism would be recognized at once as a conservative monopoly. But this is by no means what happened. Thorstein Veblen built an elaborate critique of capitalism on Darwinian premises. Lewis Henry Morgan looked beyond the property phase of human society to "a revival, in a higher form, of the liberty, equality, and fraternity of the ancient gentes." [9] Lester Frank Ward, an impassioned messiah, believed that the evolutionary hypothesis was perfectly compatible with a program for extensive social control of mankind's destiny.[10] And a plenitude of others looked for and thought they found in Darwinism a confirmation of the American dream. The new science did not, on its face, present humanitarian social theory with an unescapable dilemma. The preconceptions of democracy could be, and were, reconciled to the biologic revelation.

But they found themselves in strange company, and the alliance was never an easy one. The Darwinian apostles who took this line were intoxicated by what they seemed on the point of proving — that the postulates of American democratic faith were supported by sermons in stones, by the findings of science. They seemed unaware that in pressing this claim they endangered the very principles they strove for. By implication at least, they had conceded that democracy was *dependent* on such empirical proofs. Thus the democratic ethic was stripped of the independent, normative validity which was its tower of strength and was tied to the kite of scientism. And the association was inevitably degrading, for henceforth, unless the facts of science supported the democratic cause, the cause itself was challengeable. The claims of democracy to moral superiority were vitiated when its advocates embraced the same criteria of moral validity as its opponents. The feature of Social Darwinism that made it most devastating to democracy was not its support of the conservative position but its materialism, which — being accepted as a matter of course — undermined the arguments of the democrats.

Social Darwinism, then, played a double role in the history of American conservatism: it worked both as a champion of the business ethic and as a hidden enemy in the camp of progressive democracy. And while my present interest is chiefly in the first of these roles, it should not be forgotten that the acceptance of Darwinian social analogies by the proponents of democracy made it easier for conservatives to perform the intellectual sleight of hand that twisted the democratic ideology to their uses.

II

Such were the doctrinal raw materials out of which a new conservative rationale could be fashioned, a rationale made to the order of an age suspicious of trancendental verities and avid for empirical proofs. Post-bellum America was peculiarly vulnerable to an ideologic attack that exalted worldly success, that exploited the growing prestige of science, that appealed for verification to the tangible and the "real." Well might it be said, in the America of the 1870's, that if Malthus and Darwin had never lived, they would have had to be invented.

Nevertheless, the gospel needed its Saint Paul; it was not self-executing. The sermons must be spoken, the truths driven home, the heretics routed. Left to themselves, men might distort and misinterpret the evidence, might overlook the all-important conclusions. What was required was a man endowed by temperament and capacity to preach the new faith: one whose moral predispositions were soundly conservative, yet who disclaimed all moral predispositions; one who rightfully wore the mantle of the scholar, yet shared the simple materialism of his less-schooled contemporaries; one who would fight for what he believed like a religious zealot, yet not surrender to the sentimentality religion sometimes begets.

This mortal need was filled in part at least by William Graham Sumner (1840–1910), a clergyman turned sociologist and pamphleteer. Called in 1872 to a new Chair of Political and Social Science at Yale, Sumner occupied the next thirty-odd years pouring forth a stream of maledictions on the heads of those who, in spite of the revealed truths of Darwinism, still persisted in "the absurd effort to make the world over." These diatribes usually took the form of essays, written for popular consumption and published in the semiserious journals of the period. Many of them were perceptive and acute; a few were eloquent and persuasive; and almost all betrayed the writer's prejudices, in which *a priori* moral convictions and a stubborn affection for strictly empirical standards were strangely intertwined. Both they and their writer appear to have been enormously influential. The essays were widely distributed and much quoted; and at Yale, where the influence of Sumner's personality was felt directly, whole generations of undergraduates were "given to Sumnerology" [11]

Sumner was, in our terms, a conservative, although he would have rejected the impeachment most violently. For him, conservatism suggested a sentimental attachment to the past, a woolly-headed veneration for outmoded symbols and beliefs. It suggested, in the days when such issues still blazed, the theological backwardness of men like Noah Porter, president of Yale, who banned the study of Herbert Spencer in Sumner's classes. Sumner himself was, on the contrary, fanatically empirical, furious at orthodox restrictions on the pursuit of knowledge, contemptuous of the nonutilitarian wherever he found it. In this sense, he was a rebel. But the free inquiry for which he struggled led him to conclusions that were conservative in the only meaningful sense of the term. It led him to support, with all the resources of his considerable scholarly gifts, the right of men to acquire as much property as they liked and to do with it as they willed. It led him to criticize sharply the democratic concept of popular sovereignty and to oppose any extension of the principle. Finally, it led him to an idea of natural superiority that inevitably implied the glorification of the business leader as the modern aristocrat. Point for point, he adopted as his own the traditional presumptions of conservatism but gave them — and here is the clue to his importance — a restatement in hardheaded, materialistic, "scientific" terms, brewed to the order of the postwar generation.

By taste and temperament, as well as conviction, Sumner was a man of the Gilded Age. He was born for the era of industrial capitalism and blast furnaces; it is difficult to imagine this austere, skeptical, unimaginative spirit flourishing in another environment. His father, Thomas Sumner, whom William vastly admired, was an uneducated and generally unsuccessful facsimile of himself, frugal, hard working, tough-minded. "Subtlety of reasoning and the mystical," says Sumner's biographer, speaking of the Lancashire textile workers like Thomas Sumner, "were foreign to their practical, straightforward type of mind." [12] Such qualities were equally foreign, throughout his life, to the mind of William. He embraced the rank materialism of America in the Gilded Age, not because it was the fashion, but because it was the only language he could really understand. His father was the prototype of Sumner's "forgotten man," the repository of all the arid virtues and limitations that made up his vision of Utopia.

Sumner's early life is replete with portents of his later destiny. From almost the first we can see developing those qualities that were to equip him so nobly for the messianic task he undertook — the deep-grained prejudice in favor of the businesslike virtues, the stubborn dogmatism once a view had been formed, the distrust for the beautiful, the intangible, the "unreal." "Frivolity, waste of time, neglect of opportunity, were even in his early days abhorrent to him . . . Along with these characteristics went a pronounced tendency to criticize and reform, which made him disliked and feared." [13] So his admiring biographer tells us, and we are constrained to agree that this righteous youth must have appeared an unconscionable prig. Neither his brother nor his sister liked him much; his mother died when he was eight years old, and the stepmother who succeeded her lavished little tenderness on the children. This loveless childhood was hardly calculated to modify William's native austerity; the oddly sober boy became a man to whom the conception of human brotherhood was mawkish, who despised the soft and sentimental to the end of his days.

Already his substantive views were forming and congealing into lifetime prejudices. When he was thirteen, he found Harriet Martineau's *Illustrations* in a Hartford library and devoured it; and in 1889 we find him admitting, unbelievable as it seems, "that my conceptions of capital, labor, money, and trade, were all formed by those books which I read in my boyhood." [14] His mind appears to have closed in youth to the entry of new basic ideas, new tastes, the opinions of others. The ideas of his father about "labor agitators" and "the gospel of gush" were essentially indistinguishable from those the son later glossed over with the respectability of scholarship and science.

In 1859, Sumner entered Yale, a man "with few friends, reserved and repellent in manner, mature beyond his years, with strong moral and religious convictions, and with no ambition but to get knowledge." [15] The university was at this time a dismal place for a man seeking inspiration,[16] but Sumner seems not to have minded. He was intent on a career as a clergyman and applied himself vigorously within the limits of the narrow, set curriculum. Graduating with honors in 1863, he set off for a term of study in Europe, first at Geneva, then at Göttingen, finally at Oxford. The scholars of biblical science at Göttingen impressed him enormously; he rejoiced in their rigorous devotion to the scientific method, their disregard for any consideration except demonstrable truth.[17]

American theology at this time labored under the restraints of a confining dependence on tradition which stood in sharp contrast to the inquiring spirit of the Göttingen scholars. The matter-of-fact, empirical strain in Sumner's character was stimulated by these men as it could never have been by a mystical, poetic approach to problems of religious faith. Theology took on meaning for him as it assumed the nature of a science. But religion is not, of course, a science, and the man who wants it to be can find fulfillment only in such rare havens as the Göttingen of those days. Sumner was temperamentally unfitted for the priesthood from the first; he needed rather a medium in which his hardheaded, scientific spirit could flourish, where his distaste for metaphysical abstractions and his incomprehension of beauty would be no handicap.

It seems indeed that, in spite of the unquestioning dogmatism of his youth, religion was never an important emotional factor in Sumner's life. We may perhaps assume that he put on the robe mainly because the church at this time offered one of the few vocations open to a young man of small means and a bookish turn of mind. In 1866 he was invited to a tutorship at Yale, and his letter of acceptance is revelatory. He preferred, he said, not to bind himself for longer than a one-year term, because "after getting so expensive an education for my profession it would not pay for me now to spend two or three years in any work aside from it." [18]

He did stay, however, for three years — fretting now as he had not before under the limitations of an outworn educational tradition. He left in 1869 to resume his calling, first as assistant to the rector of Calvary Church, New York, and as editor of a fledgling magazine, *The Living Church;* later as rector of the Church of the Redeemer in Morristown, New Jersey. His sermons there are chiefly distinguished by a determined but finally unavailing effort to reconcile his religion with a growing concern for mundane affairs. The new world of science tempted him more and more; he seemed to find it less and less easy to explain in his sermons how a strict devotion to empirical truth can be conjoined with religious faith. "A conflict is impending," he said in his farewell sermon, "between the traditional dogmas and modern speculation and science in which it is possible that all religion may be lost . . . The great question is whether there is an historical revelation of spiritual and universal truths which has authority for man, or whether each man and each generation must reason out the whole problem afresh, or rest contented with so much knowledge of himself as he can win through the senses." [19]

Then the call to the new chair at Yale came to relieve him of encircling doubts and to resolve the conflict between the empiricist and the clergyman. Those doubts, that conflict, had been aggravated not a little by the reading of Herbert Spencer's recently published *The Study of Sociology* (1873). The book revived dreams of Oxford days when Sumner's first contact with the works of Henry Thomas Buckle had led him to hope that men might construct a true science of society. For Sumner thought of himself, throughout most of his life, as a man with a mission. There was little enough of the Olympian about this earthbound spirit in most ways, but in one sense at least his conception was grandiose: he looked forward to the day when the immutable laws of society would be all revealed and he and others like him might confront the erring multitude with irrefutable proof of its folly.

The return to Yale, in fact, resolved his spiritual as well as his professional dilemma with a finality that even he did not realize at the time. Much later he said: "I never consciously gave up a religious belief. It was as if I had put my beliefs into a drawer, and when I opened it there was nothing there at all." [20] The faith of his father could not survive in the world of cold fact where Sumner henceforth dwelt — or thought he dwelt, which is the really significant thing.

It is important in tracing the intellectual development of the man to note that his retreat from religion took this form. One by one, as he ventured into new realms of knowledge, the external symbols of religious belief — God, scriptural authority, the idea of personal immortality — sloughed away almost unobserved. But vestiges survived, all the more persistent because he was unaware of their dependence on a formal religious system. If at any given point Sumner had expressly abjured the faith of his youth, he might have proceeded forthwith to a reëxamination of all its premises. Under the circumstances, no such thoroughgoing soul-search took place, and he retained as semiconscious prejudices a set of dogmas that had once been articles of spiritual faith.

From the religious training of his youth, for example, he derived — and forever retained — his notion of human virtue, a notion reinforced by his father's own character and quality. The good man was chaste, frugal, industrious, and devoted to duty; he walked alone, secure in the certainty of rectitude, and mended his own fences — in short, he was the ideal parishioner in the church of Cotton Mather. There was no humor about this paragon, no frivolity, very little charity. It was no coincidence that Sumner later discovered a natural order wherein these virtues were the prerequisite of survival and success.

And this concept of natural order itself was no less an afterglow of entrenched religious convictions. In his search for a rational law of social development, Sumner discarded many a truth that had been regarded as self-evident, but he retained for a long time the assumption that there was such a law, that it was perceptible to human reason, and that it worked in general toward benevolent ends. This preconception, so typical of the nineteenth-century mind, was nothing more than the idea of a divine plan with the divinity left out. It was easy for Sumner and many of his contemporaries to drop the hypothesis of God; it was more difficult for them to abandon the hypothesis of Order.

Sumner lived in an age of waning spiritual vitality, an era in which empiricism won some impressive triumphs. This fact is worth noting, but the period cannot be understood if we assume that religious faith was divested like a suit of clothes and that the new empiricist stood forth naked. Sumner's ideal man was a Puritan survival, and he differed from his earlier prototype mainly in that a supernatural sanction for his character was no longer considered necessary. His qualities were, or seemed, familiar, and indeed their familiarity was an essential element of their appeal. But what was apparent neither to Sumner nor his contemporaries was that, without spiritual sanction, the ideal emerged a poor creature. Deprived of the moral support of a God who had decreed his virtues, the Sumnerian man became the Hobbesian man, amoral, egoistic, and meaningless. The notion of a fundamental law of nature suffered a like fate. Deprived of its association with the Divinity and reduced to strictly materialist terms, the concept of natural order was converted into a cold and sterile determinism. A beneficent or malevolent end was equally likely; the only certainty was that no human agency could direct the result. Nevertheless, it was for Sumner a dogmatic certainty like all his basic convictions, which were as dependable and unarguable as the revealed truth that science had taught him to forswear.

Sumner's native distaste for the nonuseful, the beautiful, is nowhere better revealed than in his crusade for a new standard in higher education. When he took his chair at Yale, the utilitarian revolution in American colleges was already under way. In his inaugural address in 1869, President Eliot of Harvard had sounded the clarion call for the elective sys-

tem and set going a movement that Spencer foresaw was to
result in "the triumph of science over art and literature." [21]
Sumner entered the fray on behalf of science without hesitation. There can be little doubt that the traditional college
curriculum needed revision at this time. It ran in a narrow
groove of orthodoxy that set intolerable limitations on the
range of human knowledge. But Sumner was not, by temperament or conviction, a man who could be expected to take
a moderate position on such a question. The baby went out
with the bathwater; the classical tradition was attacked at
all points. He objected to the disutility of requiring one of
his sons, destined for a business career, to learn Greek as a
prerequisite for entrance to Yale College. "It has been
claimed for the classics that they give guidance for conduct,"
he said. "This is to me the most amazing claim of all, for in
my experience and observation, the most marked fact about
classical culture is that it gives no guidance in conduct at
all." [22] The remark is an apt enough illustration of Sumner's
inner contempt for aesthetic and cultural values. What he
meant, of course, was that the classics are of no help in the
business of making a living, that they can have little relevance
in the life of that ideal forgotten man for whom society was
ordained. The imperatives of conduct were summarized for
Sumner in the catalogue of virtues he had ascribed to his
ideal. The trappings of what is ordinarily called "culture"
are at best superfluous. At worst, they are "the greatest barrier to new ideas and the chief bulwark of modern obscur-
antism." [23]

Sumner never left Yale, although his quarrel with President Porter over Spencer tempted him to do so. For twenty
years his major preoccupation was economics, a subject he
taught with a zest and dogmatism that made him extraordinarily popular among his students. As time wore on, however,
his interest began to shift to the nascent field of sociology,

and in the nineties he abandoned his undergraduate courses in economics altogether. Henceforth the "science of society" absorbed him, and it is to his work in this field that he owes his academic reputation.

Meanwhile, his published works had steadily piled up: a series of studies in American economic history; biographies of Jackson, Hamilton, and Robert Morris; and — most important from the point of view of this study — a great spate of essays and articles in which he aired his opinions on the social and economic problems of the day. When we add the *Folkways* and *The Science of Society* it is an impressive enough list, but a catalogue of the works themselves is not enough to explain the strong influence he undoubtedly exerted on the American mind. His prose style was always spotty and sometimes downright clumsy. His logical power was not great; even the short essays are often discursive and lacking in cohesion. The *sequiturs* are frequently hard to find. And in spite of his protestations to the contrary, there is a continual slipping back and forth between empiricism and moral judgment. He was contemptuous of soft-minded social reformers, but he could not conceal, even from himself, the fact that he too was a zealot, a salesman of ideas and of a kind of social reform. In *The Forgotten Man and Other Essays* he says, speaking of protectionism: "The moral indignation which it causes is the motive that draws me away from the scientific pursuits which form my real occupation and forces me to take part in popular agitation." [24] But as a result his polemical writing, with all its purported dependence on hard, irrefutable fact, is curiously unconvincing to the reader who is not predisposed to agree with him, who is not seized by the same moral indignation. His occasional flashes of real insight, his sometimes impressive gift for memorable statement, are easy to pass over in reaction against the cocksure dogmatism that pervades almost everything he wrote.

But these observations, together with our consideration of his intellectual development, contain the answer to the riddle of his influence. Those who read Sumner's essays and agreed with them were not seeking an idea; they were seeking a rationalization. It was enough that he articulated some of their own felt convictions, that he coated their prejudices with the varnish of logic and academic respectability. Moreover, Sumner's intellectual history, his steady adherence to material values and proofs made him a reflection in vignette of the Gilded Age itself. The age too had put religious faith in the drawer; it too had exalted the materialist virtues; it too worshiped "the bitch goddess"; it too canonized the man of business affairs. Sumner was ideally suited to provide post-bellum conservatism with what it required — a new justification of its basic aims harmonious with the new political and economic and cultural context.

A study of William Graham Sumner is then, in a very real sense, a study of his era, and the nature of the new conservative rationale is revealed with unique clarity in his works. There are two reasons, beyond those already suggested, for assigning Sumner this special status in the American conservative tradition. In the first place he is, among contemporary spokesmen of the cause, the one who most nearly merits the title of political philosopher. As we shall see, the designation is not very apt; Sumner himself would not have chosen it. But he had read fairly widely in the field of political theory; he was familiar with some of the problems in that area that had bedeviled men for centuries; and, as a consequence, he felt an obligation to deal in somewhat formal terms with certain central theoretical issues. Thus it may fairly be said that Sumner gives us the most nearly rounded statement of the conservative position. He works it out in some detail, as a scholar must, and goes beyond the confines of the mere special pleader. In the second place, Sumner's native hardheadedness led him to accept and follow through, as few others would, the full implication of his premises. Others might talk of "nature red in tooth and claw" and "the survival of the fittest," but in varying degrees they flinched from stating all the harsh conclusions that logically ensued from these precepts. Sumner was troubled by no such fastidious scruples. He hewed to the line of his argument and spelled out its results, scornful of euphemism. Therefore, when we consider Sumner, we confront the new conservatism in what comes closest to being its natural state; we are seeing it for what it is rather than for what ambiguity can make it. Sumner offered a vision of society in which beauty, charity, and brotherhood could find no place, in which wealth and self-interest were the ruling norms. And this was the social ideal the age embraced when it accepted Sumner's postulates.

three

CAPITALISM, SUMNERISM, AND DEMOCRACY

I

William Graham Sumner, then, supplied the premises for what came to be known as "the gospel of wealth"; he was the schoolmaster, the grammarian, of the new conservatism. And in order to understand the root nature of the credo, it becomes necessary to examine those premises in some detail.

Enough has been said already to indicate that Sumner did not wipe his mental slate clean of prejudice when he set himself the task of developing a science of society. He brought to that enterprise a mind instinctively hostile to abstract formulations of ethical principles and contemptuous of the metaphysical and the intangible. But he brought also a set of ideals gleaned largely from the model of his father and his Puritan heritage. Even more important, he brought a deep-seated predisposition to moralize, to defend virtue and castigate evil. Sumner had not abandoned either *a priorism* or ethicism; he had simply abandoned the spiritual faith which had supported his *a priori* ethical assumptions.

These facts are crucial to an understanding of the man and the doctrine he preached. For the core of his thought is his ethic, his idea of the good. Sumner's view of capitalism and the capitalist, of progress, the state, and democracy, are all ultimately dependent on an unstated, but nevertheless pervasive, ethical premise. And it was this criterion of value that he imposed on the nascent conservative tradition.

II

Though it would have infuriated him to be told so, Sumner's ethical position emerges most clearly in that most scientific and scholarly of his works, the *Folkways*. Like so many positivists, Sumner denied that his system of thought rested on a postulate of ultimate value. For him morality was, as he said in the *Folkways*, "historical, institutional, and empirical," that is, always relative to time and place.[1] Therefore, "the introduction of ethical notions or dogmas can never do anything but obscure the study of the facts and relations which alone should occupy attention."[2] Nevertheless, when we look more closely we perceive that the matter is not so simple as this. Behind the observation that morality is epiphenomenal and the position of professed moral relativism that ensues, we can see the outlines of an operative value standard. This standard, as has been suggested, becomes most nearly explicit in the *Folkways*, but it is clear that it did not originate there. We can project it back into the essays, back to the day when Sumner put his religious faith in the drawer, back to the time when he first took up the cudgel against sentimentalism and social reform. Whenever, in his writings, Sumner advocated or denounced, he did so on the basis of an implied theory of right and wrong that is indistinguishable from the "scientific" norm he espoused in the *Folkways*.

The formulation by which he arrived at that norm was, in its essence, simple enough: In the beginning there are four great motives common to men — hunger, love, vanity, and fear.[3] The motives give rise to interests, and, in an attempt to satisfy them, men adopt modes of action which have been shown by experience to serve the purpose best. For example, a certain technique in hunting is learned to be the "right" way by a process of trial and error. Since men are similar in needs and capacities, this rightness for one man has a tendency to become rightness for all, especially if environmental conditions are similar. Of course, the supposed lesson learned from experience may be a false one.[4] Ghost-fear and goblinism may lead to an erroneous calculation,[5] and other factors may play a part in producing aberrant folkways. Nonetheless, an idea of expediency, however wrong-headed, provides the original drive.

So far the folkways are merely habitual ways of doing things, of satisfying interests, ways that experience seems to show are expedient. At some point, however, the "elements of truth and right" thus empirically derived are generalized into a theory of societal welfare, and the folkways become "mores." "The mores are the customs in which life is held when taken together with the moral judgments as to the bearing of the same on welfare." [6]

The objective of a custom that has attained the status of an ethical imperative is then societal welfare. The inference men make about what conduct is useful to society determines the inference they will make about what conduct is morally right. Unfortunately, we find that this process, like the process of creating the original folkways, "has been liable to most pernicious errors . . . men have turned their backs on welfare and reality, in order to pursue beauty, glory, poetry, and dithyrambic rhetoric." [7] These false values enter in at the second stage of the act-thought-act sequence and give rise to error concerning what is actually the conduct best calculated to serve societal welfare. That is, the "prevailing world philosophy" suggests inferences which then become entangled with and pervert the correct judgment of expediency. Especially, "speculative assumptions and dogmatic deductions have produced the mischief here described." [8]

The use of terms in these passages is highly significant.

The position of ethical relativism which Sumner assumes when he says repeatedly that the mores "can make anything right" [9] is hardly consistent with the use of such words as "mischief" and "error" in evaluating the mores at any given time. If "right" and "wrong" have no meaning apart from their definition in the mores, then it is obvious nonsense to speak of the mores themselves as "good" or "bad." Yet Sumner has no hesitation in so describing them.[10] Evidently, there is a standard for judging the mores apart from themselves, a norm which is presumed to be in some sense independently valid.

The term Sumner uses to describe that norm is "societal welfare." Mores are good when they actually subserve that end, bad when they do not. Ideals are useful when they are directed toward the attainment of welfare, pernicious when they are misdirected. Yet there is obviously something still missing. For "societal welfare" is itself only a phrase and, until it is given content, cannot serve as a basis of judgment. Being defined by the mores, it can hardly be helpful in evaluating them. It is incumbent on Sumner then to explain what he means by "societal welfare," and in examining that explanation we approach the real nub of the *Folkways'* ethics.

Some hint of the meaning Sumner assigned to this term can be inferred from what has already been said and from a consideration of the elements that had, for Sumner, societal value. Evidently "beauty, glory, poetry, and dithyrambic rhetoric" lack such value, since they are listed among the "pernicious errors" which may enter in at the second stage of the act-thought-act sequence. Apparently, too, philosophical and ethical ideals can have no societal utility, since they are mere means which more or less adequately serve the social objective. At their best — that is, when they really conduce to welfare — "the scope of achievement in the satisfaction of needs is enormously extended." But "when the mores go wrong it is, above all, on account of error in the attempt to employ the philosophical and ethical generalizations in order to impose upon mores and institutions a movement towards selected and 'ideal' results . . . Then the energy of the society may be diverted from its interests . . . energy is expended on acts which are contrary to welfare." [11] Beauty and ethical ideals then are valuable only insofar as they subserve societal welfare. And, since they bear this dependent relationship to welfare, they obviously cannot be among its constituents.

So much for what "societal welfare" is not. The discovery of what it is involves the disentanglement of some nettling ambiguities. Sumner hesitated to give the concept explicit definition, although he sometimes approached doing so. "What is true," he tells us, "is that there are periods of social advance and periods of social decline, that is, advance or decline in *economic power, material prosperity,* and *group strength for war.*" [12] Elsewhere, he presents us with a population curve based on the societal-value criterion and suggests that such value conforms, albeit imperfectly, to "worldly success and to income from work contributed to the industrial organization." [13] This standard does not altogether satisfy him, and he immediately hedges it slightly by confessing that scientific and artistic works are sometimes underpriced. Nevertheless, he believes that in general the criterion holds, and that social value can be fairly accurately measured in terms of this strictly material and economic norm. That Sumner himself accepted the validity of such a norm is hardly disputable. The references to art and culture in the broader sense have invariably the character of afterthoughts. Throughout the *Folkways* and his other writings as well, the great weight of emphasis falls on the economic criterion in resolving issues of good or evil. It is most significant that nowhere in Sumner's works does he acknowledge a situation in which considerations of economic welfare might be overridden by other, less material, societal concerns.

What we have here then is a social ethic that is utilitarian in the narrowest possible sense. Not only are moral questions subservient to expediency, but expediency itself is defined strictly in terms of material, economic objectives. Beauty, humanitarianism, liberty — all these are secondary to the supreme normative consideration: economic prosperity and power. It must be emphasized that Sumner has here gone far beyond his original insight that ideas of right and wrong arise from a primitive judgment of expediency. This is an anthropologic observation which may or may not be sound, but which in itself suggests nothing in particular about the final moral validity of those ideas. Sumner has taken the much greater step of setting up a transcendent standard of goodness and badness; he has established an absolute materialist ethic.

And this ethic provides the principle for judging questions of social policy and individual behavior; it supplies both the social and personal ideals. A "right" social policy is one that conduces to the material welfare of society, and a "wrong" social policy is the converse. Likewise, the good man must be he who contributes to society's material welfare; a man who does not so contribute or who in any way hampers material progress is, by definition, bad. Thus the operating virtues approved by the Sumnerian ethic are those that promote material well-being, and from here — given the assumptions of classical economics and Social Darwinism — it is a simple step to say that the good man is he who most single-mindedly seeks to promote *his own* well-being. Selfishness is raised to the status of an absolute good; the Hobbesian man becomes the moral ideal.

With this ethical understructure firmly in mind, we are in a position to go on to examine some of the notions about capitalism, the state, progress, and democracy that Sumner derived from his basic value assumption.

III

As has already been suggested, the ethical premise just described did not originate for Sumner in his study of folkways. Long before, he had given it implied but unmistakable expression in his polemical writings and had, what is more, worked out its logical consequences in some detail. It is the essays, then, which prove beyond any lingering doubt that in Sumner's theory the concept of societal welfare is not a merely contingent scientific yardstick (like Pareto's "utility to the community"), but a full-fledged value standard. Nowhere is this more clearly underlined than in the supreme value Sumner assigned to capital accumulation as the *sine qua non* of social advance.

Sumner had one very simple idea about "capital," and that idea, simple though it is, pervades his whole theory of society and controls his every judgment about the social order. He thought that capital was the primary index of social improvement, "the instrumentality by which, from the beginning, man has won and held every step of this development of civilization." [14] "The only two things which really tell on the welfare of man on earth are hard work and self-denial (in technical language, labor and capital), and these tell most when they are brought to bear directly upon the effort to earn an honest living, to accumulate capital, and to bring up a family of children to be industrious and self-denying in their turn." [15] The aggregation of capital, therefore, is the highest social good.

It follows, on Sumner's premises, that the man who accumulates capital is serving society and serving it in the only meaningful sense of the term. The harder he works to lay away his little hoard, the more self-denying he is, the more virtuously he is behaving. Attacks on accumulators of capital are therefore the utmost folly, since to attack them is to undermine civilization itself.[16] It is nonsense to suggest that only the owner of capital enjoys its benefits, for the usufruct, except for a small margin, passes on to the community as a whole.[17]

Yet even if it be granted, as Sumner explicitly states,[18] "that the savings bank depositor is a hero of civilization," there might still be room to doubt that the aggregation of capital in a few hands is wholly beneficent. Agitators in Sumner's day were in arms, not against the frugal workingman, but against the millionaire; not against bank deposits, but against "trusts." If Sumner was to spell out a rounded defense of post-bellum American capitalism, he was bound to justify its excessive concentration of wealth. He had to demonstrate not only that capital itself was a good thing, but that its virtual monopoly by a small minority was desirable. In meeting this issue, Sumner drew on the general premises of Social Darwinism and upon his own purportedly inductive conclusions regarding the existence of a natural elite.

The argument from Social Darwinism was the elementary one that, if the social and economic order is left to run itself, the fittest will survive, and among them those who are most capable will gain the greatest advantage. Fitness, on Sumner's postulates, means of course fitness to contribute to the material welfare of society. "Let it be understood that we cannot go outside of this alternative: liberty, inequality, survival of the fittest; not — liberty, equality, survival of the unfittest. The former carries society forward and favors all its best members; the latter carries society downwards and favors all its worst members." [19] It is true that unregulated entrepreneurship will produce millionaires and monopolists. But this is not to be regretted.

It is idle folly to meet these phenomena with wailings about the danger of the accumulation of great wealth in few hands. The phenomena themselves prove that we have tasks to perform which require large aggregations of capital. Moreover, the capital, to be effective, must be in few hands, for the simple reason that there are very few men who are able to handle great aggregations of capital . . . The men who are competent to organize great enterprises and to handle great amounts of capital must be found by natural selection, not by political election . . . The aggregation of large amounts of capital in few hands is the first condition of the fulfilment of the most important tasks of civilization which now confront us.[20]

If we should set a limit to the accumulation of wealth, we should say to our most valuable producers, "We do not want you to do us the services which you best understand how to perform, beyond a certain point." It would be like killing off our generals in war.[21]

Great inequalities of wealth therefore are not only to be tolerated; they are to be encouraged. The free working of the market will produce monopolists. Those monopolists will attempt to impose their will on society in the form of plutocracy.[22] A certain amount of abject poverty and misery are to be expected.[23] But all these seeming evils must be endured, so that society can enjoy the benefits which the millionaire showers upon it.[24]

The elitist concept enunciated in the *Folkways* merges with and supports the Social Darwinist argument. I have already referred to Sumner's use of a population curve based on a hypothetical standard of societal value.[25] Men of genius and talent — "the classes" — are distinguished from the great body of mediocrities — "the masses" — and both are distinguished from the unskilled and illiterate, the proletariat, and the defective, dependent, and delinquent elements that constitute the dregs of society. The men of genius and talent are, of course, a very small minority, while "the masses" are the vast majority; yet it is "the classes" who have historically been responsible for advances in societal welfare, who have supplied the answers to "the problem of life." [26] It may be that the classes have supplied those answers under the spur of selfish motivations, but this is irrelevant. They must be left free to pursue their ends, because only they can introduce changes in the mores which will carry society ahead.

Now an argument that takes these directions must inevitably issue in a glorification of the successful businessman as such. He and his fellows constitute the anointed elite of the social order Sumner is describing, and no amount of incidental qualification of this main judgment can change its central character. Sumner is not altogether happy about this conclusion. Temperamentally he seems to have admired most, not the millionaire, but the hard-working, self-sufficient, middle-class paragon whom his essays eulogize.[27] He speaks in disapproving terms of "the elevation of success to a motive which justified itself," both in our own society and in the Italian renaissance.[28] He abhorred plutocracy, which involves the use of industrial power for political ends.[29] As even he could see, the Sumnerian virtues of industry, frugality, and self-reliance were not always exemplified by the Goulds and Fisks of his era.[30] But he was caught in the toils of his own argument, as conservative theory itself has been caught ever since.

For by the terms of that argument the Protestant virtues do not justify themselves; they are justified because they promote the material welfare of society, and they are therefore dependent on that standard. Material value is the controlling norm, and since, by definition, the best measure of such value is success, the successful businessman is meritorious whether he practices Sumner's Protestant virtues or not. The more he aggregates wealth, the more the industrialist serves the community; and the methods he employs are morally unimpeachable because no moral standard for impeaching them exists. Sumner himself by no means felt that the successful businessman could do no wrong, but in criticizing unscrupulous profit-chasing he was trying to have the best of two contrasting value systems, and on his own premises he was clearly astray. The logic of his materialist ethic was to exalt "the man who can do things" to the level of social heroism.

IV

Sumner was in most respects incorrigibly a skeptic, a pessimist, and iconoclast. He had no patience with the bright dreams of a millennium which beguiled the Utopian school of the Social Darwinists. Poverty and misery are not temporary evils which may eventually be abolished; they are rather nature's harsh sanction against the vices inherent in human nature; they maintain the vitality of the social body in the same way that antibodies maintain the health of the individual.[31] And just as the abolition of known disease might debilitate the human organism and make it susceptible to the ravages of some new plague, so the end of poverty would encourage sloth in the social system and would lead inevitably to its degeneration.[32]

Back of this grim determinism that condemned the social order to chronic ailment, there was of course a profound conviction that human nature is incapable of basic improvement, a conviction that may well have been related to the concept of original sin in the theological system Sumner thought he had cast aside. Such an assumption is ultimately unprovable; it must rest upon an intuition. Yet Sumner, with his declared distaste for *a priorism*, states it in the form of an absolute truth.

At any rate, whatever the psychological origins of such a notion may have been, Sumner himself did not fully accept its implications. He did not, as it seems he logically might have, reject altogether the possibility of social improvement. Progress — albeit of a very limited kind — can be made and is apparently worth striving for.

But what Sumner meant by the word "progress" can be inferred from the discussion of his other concepts. It meant to him "winning more social power"; it was "increased by all improvements in any department of industrial effort." [33] In short, it meant material advance, the accumulation of capital goods. The problem of social improvement for Sumner boils down, therefore, to the question of what action can be taken to encourage the development of capital and thereby ensure the progress of man.

To begin with, it is clear that any proposed action must conform to the state of the mores, which in turn have a rough correspondence to "life conditions." The mores sometimes fall out of harmony with those conditions, in which case there is a slow but insistent tendency for them to readapt themselves, to strain toward improvement and consistency.[34] Against this tendency, however, is the natural inertia of the mores, their characteristic resistance to change. Institutions then can be altered only within the limits of these conditioning factors. They cannot be altered in defiance of the mores, hence they cannot be modified to accord with ideal ends. They cannot be altered quickly, hence the absurdity of all schemes to make the world over. The role of conscious human effort, the function of the social scientist, is to discover what social arrangements will best serve the needs of material welfare and to labor to shape institutions in accord with those needs, always conforming any proposal, however, to the limitations imposed by the mores. The social thinker may usefully attack false mores when he sees them developing, and it is his duty to criticize those mores that have outgrown their usefulness (that is, their correspondence to society's physical needs). But his function is at best neutral and negative: it consists in discovering the drift of history and removing impediments to its fulfillment. By hypothesis, the basic direction cannot be changed.[35]

It will be seen that the doctrine of progress which Sumner derived from his study of folkways was in its essence profoundly conservative. It was, in fact, something very like a statement in scientific terminology of the principles and sentiments of Edmund Burke. Existing institutions have the same postulated appropriateness for the society in which they have grown; they are rooted in the historical process; and they resist arbitrary change.[36] The great difference is of course that, in place of Burke's sentimental and almost religious veneration for the authority of the past, Sumner had substituted a positivistic ethic — the morality of material survival.

Clearly then, the mores set limits to the scope of societal improvement, and the function of the social scientist, the expert, is correspondingly restricted. But what is it that provides the impetus to carry society forward within these limits? Supposing progress to be possible at all, how is it achieved? The answer, for Sumner, was clear. Progress is attained by the accumulation of capital, which in turn is made possible by "labor, toil, self-denial and study" [37] in a regime of freedom under contract, of competition, of struggle and survival.[38] In short, progress is achieved, not by deliberate planning and choice, but through the force of mutual selfishness of individuals.

These propositions add up to little more, of course, than the "invisible hand" of the classical economists, together with the shibboleths of Sumner's Social Darwinism. Yet obviously, even if the validity of the argument so far is conceded, there is something missing. It can be granted that no extreme reforms are possible because of the stickiness of the mores; it can be granted that the accumulation of capital is best accomplished by individual effort. But it remains to be proved that the state should play no part at all in the social task, that it should not actively participate in the business world so as to increase the community's capital increment. If such measures were undertaken with a due care that they conform to the mores and to social laws, they would seem to be beneficent by Sumner's own standards. Above all, it is hard to see why the state should not take a hand when the competitive process is perverted, when the formation of monopolies and trusts actually sets the social laws in abeyance. Yet Sumner, true to his role as the spokesman of the new conservatism, was bitterly opposed to both such kinds of governmental meddling. It was necessary for him to explain then why private activity was the only sort that could serve the societal purpose, and this explanation rested upon his concept of the nature and function of the state.

V

As might be expected, Sumner troubled himself very little over metaphysical and ethical problems in formulating his view of the state. The traditional issues of political philosophy seemed to him largely irrelevant; they dissolved in the presence of his Yankee "common sense." Thus he was afflicted by none of the problems that involved his contemporary, Spencer, in such a mass of contradictions, because he had, for example, no idealist concept of an organismic state to reconcile with his scientism. Such preconceptions as he had were unconscious, and this relieved him of the obligation to defend them.[39]

His idea of the state, therefore, must be drawn largely from negative arguments whose main import is to show that the state is incapable of positive action to stimulate social progress. The theory of the state, important though it looms in Sumner's thought, is actually incidental to the argument for "laissez faire." This argument consists of two related propositions.

In the first place, Sumner argued that society is a vast and extraordinarily complex mechanism of interrelated parts and that action at any given point will produce a multitude of reactions at other remote points in the mechanism. He was acutely conscious that the science of society was in its infancy and that it called for exhaustive study of interacting phenomena that so far "defy analysis." [40] He was perhaps more than ever conscious of this after his own monumental and painstaking investigation of folkways, and it disturbed him that, in the face of such difficulties, the "social tinker" would yet undertake to cure social disorders. "The student of sociology as a science will necessarily feel a great timidity about all generalization. There are so many more things that he does not know than there are which he does know." [41] Yet the social meddler "regards all the displacement which he can accomplish as positively new creation; he does not notice at all, and probably is not trained to perceive, the reaction — the other side of the change." [42]

Now this is by no means an uncompelling argument, and it sets up such a strong proof of the finite character of human wisdom that Sumner might have been content to rest his anti-state argument at this point. But there is further evidence to be brought in to drive the wedge even deeper home. Not only is the social machine too intricate for even the most learned to tamper with; there is reason to believe that the political state is peculiarly ill adapted for such a task. And it is mainly in the course of his discussion of this proposition that Sumner's ideas of the state and democratic government are set forth.

At first blush, it is apparent that the state cannot be expected to offer very much in the way of either wisdom or virtue. Stripped of metaphysical nonsense about it, the state stands forth as nothing more than "All-of-Us," and its wisdom or right can be no greater than that of the individuals who compose it. Far from possessing metaphysical properties that lift it above mundane limitations, the state is by the very nature of its constitution a fallible and inferior creation.[43] And this deduced conclusion of state incompetency can be inductively established from the facts of anthropology and history.

For one thing, the state tends, by a law of its development, to become an instrument of aggrandizement in the hands of the most powerful class in the political community. This almost purely Marxist interpretation of the state's role is historically demonstrable. "Chiefs, kings, priests, warriors, statesmen, and other functionaries have put their own interests in the place of group interests, and have used the authority they possessed to force the societal organization to work and fight for their interests." [44] "The interests of the society or nation furnishes an easy phrase, but such phrases are to be regarded with suspicion. Such interests are apt to be the interests of a ruling clique which the rest are to be compelled to serve." [45]

This organization of force for group selfishness has been characteristic of states historically, and there is no reason for supposing that recent events have altered their fundamental nature. Great forces have indeed been at work. The strict subordination of man to man which existed in societies of the past was a necessity for group protection, but as conditions of comparative peace and security have been established, the original excuse for sharp differences in status and privilege has become meaningless. Such distinctions can then be preserved only if the man-land ratio favors their maintenance — that is, if there is a relative scarcity of land and a relative abundance of labor. In the fifteenth and sixteenth centuries, the discovery of the Americas vastly increased the potentially usable land area of the globe and set in motion a historical tendency away from status relationships and aristocracy and toward contractual relationships and democracy.[46] This tendency gradually gathered force during the next three hundred years, but reached irresistible proportions only when an advance in the industrial arts, particularly those of transportation, had made the New World potential of cheap and abundant land a reality. The masses were now in a favorable bargaining position. In the past the laborer was forced to accept such terms as the class ruler offered, even if those terms involved subjection and slavery, because the labor commodity which constituted the worker's stock in trade was a drug on the market. With the situation reversed, the laborer was freed from dependence on the landowner's will; the worker could drive favorable bargains or could, alternatively, become an owner himself. A regime of freedom under contract ensued, a form of societal organization, said Sumner, which produces "by far the strongest society which has ever yet existed." [47]

A profound change in the economic circumstances, then, has radically altered the structure of modern society. But the movement gives no cause for revising the basic estimate regarding the perversity and incompetence of the political state; on the contrary, it provides grounds for confirming that estimate and even strengthening it. For the same forces that produced freedom under contract have stimulated the growth of political democracy.[48] They have given birth, that is, to a set of political dogmas which, if carried to extremes, may undo the gains established by the shift from status to contract. The dogma of political equality produces the dogma of majority rule, and the old monarchical claim to arbitrary power is transferred to the popular majority. Hence the danger almost inevitably arises in a democracy that the state will be perverted to "a system of favoring a new privileged class of the many and the poor." [49] On the other hand, there is the equally grave danger that the modern representative state will be captured by the capitalist class and transformed into a plutocracy.[50] As the nineteenth century has progressed, democracy has found it more and more difficult to resist these twin tendencies, either of which would be fatal to the regime of economic liberty which is, for Sumner, society's only salvation. He fears that a class conflict between capitalism and the proletariat will soon write an end to centuries of societal development.[51]

Class war eventuating in class dictatorship is, however, only the most dramatic of the perils inherent in the democratic idea, the end product of the modern tragic fallacy. Democracy in practice has shown itself prey to lesser ills which must weigh against it in any accounting of its capacities. The fear of one-man power is, for example, a democratic obsession, so that the people are willing to sacrifice governmental efficiency in a misguided effort to guard against such power. Irrationally, American democracy has taken refuge in the long ballot and in the arbitrary division of administrative authority between a number of independent officials. It has opposed any extension of the area of executive discretion, although the increasing diversity of governmental concerns makes such discretion imperative to effective state action.[52]

The spoils system in civil service is an unavoidable conclusion of democratic premises regarding political equality. The idea that each man is as good as the next leads to rotation in administrative office and foments stubborn popular opposition to the development of a merit system. This opens the way to the establishment of a self-perpetuating political oligarchy, since the political organizer is paid for his services in the coinage of government jobs.[53]

Democracy has also led increasingly to a new and degraded form of political decision-making. "The activity of the State, under the new democratic system, shows itself every year more at the mercy of clamorous factions, and legislators find themselves constantly under greater pressure to act, not by their deliberate judgment of what is expedient, but in such a way as to quell clamor, although against their judgment of public interests." [54] Inevitably, "the consequence is the immense power of the lobby, and legislation comes to be an affair of coalition between interests to make up a majority." [55]

The folly and danger of schemes to promote social welfare by state action must now be clear. The complexity and interdependence of society make it necessary that the formulators of such programs possess extraordinary wisdom and insight, combined with a single-minded desire to serve the general good. It is doubtful whether anyone, at the present stage of inquiry, knows enough to fulfill this requirement; it is certain that state officials in a democracy, elected on a haphazard basis by an ill-informed electorate or appointed as a reward for political services, could not, with the best intentions, remotely approach this ideal. And devotion to the public welfare is an even scarcer commodity in democratic government. The drive for power among conflicting interests tends always to convert the state into a prize to be won by the dominant class; meanwhile, issues of social policy are decided, not on the basis of their merits, but in accordance with the pressures brought to bear on the tribunes of the people. To entrust the adjustment of the delicate social mechanism to such soiled and incompetent hands would be madness.

This is the burden of Sumner's view of the state and of his arguments against state interference in social and industrial affairs. A great many of his essays and scattered paragraphs in the *Folkways* are devoted to variations on the theme. Even to a not especially sympathetic observer it seems a fairly strong case; and if Sumner's ubiquitous master standard of material welfare be accepted as the norm, the indictment is even more telling. But an examination of the argument leads to the suggestion that he wrought even better than he knew. Like Mark Twain in his "Medieval Romance," Sumner has argued himself into a cul-de-sac from which nothing but miraculous intervention can save him. Always most impressive in a destructive role, he has punctured balloons and smashed icons in a spirit worthy of his modern admirer, H. L. Mencken. But, as with Mencken, his constructive offerings are singularly unsatisfying by comparison.

He is clear enough concerning the course that should be followed in view of the state's inherent failings and the special incompetence of the democratic state. "Society needs first of all to be freed from these meddlers — that is, to be let alone. Here we are, then, once more back at the old doctrine — *Laissez faire.*" [56] Let us "minimize to the utmost the relations of the state to industry." [57] Let the state make it its business to guarantee a citizen that "in doing his best to learn the laws of right living and to obey them, to the end that his life may be a success, no one else shall be allowed to interfere with him or to demand a share in the product of his efforts." [58] And to ensure that the state shall limit itself to such a function and not be perverted to antisocial uses, "the task of constitutional government is to devise institutions which shall come into play at the critical periods to prevent the abusive control of the powers of a state by the controlling classes in it." [59] By "institutions" he means negative constitutional restraints. "On the side of political machinery there is no ground for hope, but only for fear. On the side of constitutional guarantees and the independent action of self-governing freemen there is every ground for hope." [60] Thus did Sumner call the American judiciary to its duty.

But considering Sumner's own analysis of its nature, what conceivable reason is there for believing that the state will practice such self-denial, what real justification is there for even hoping that it will? He himself tells us that "the philosophical drift in the mores of our time is toward state regulation." [61] He has represented the state as typically the tool of class interests and has emphasized the persistence of the will to power by one class or another. A comparison between his view of these matters and the ideas of Marx is naturally suggested: the concepts of economic causation are clearly related, as are the notions of the state as an instrument of class domination. But Marx maintains a consistency of viewpoint; the state in his theory retains its exploitative character to the end and finally is employed as the tool of the triumphant proletariat. Sumner fears such an eventuality, but holds out the hope that minimization of state activity will somehow preclude it. The hope may or may not be well founded, but there is nothing in Sumner's own reasoning to suggest that it is.

In the second place, what chance is there that a system of constitutional limitations, however ingeniously devised, can operate to prevent the "abusive control" of the state's powers? Sumner's whole position is a denial of the proposition that legal institutions can control the drift of economic forces.[62] He scouts the notion that the American founding fathers established democratic institutions; those institutions established themselves as a consequence of economic conditions in the New World. I have already referred to his assumption of the near-impossibility of bringing about changes that run against the mores.[63] "Legislation and preaching" are particularly ineffective.[64] Yet it is the mores, not constitutional phrases or systems, that determine the scope and character of state action.

The fact is that Sumner was torn between a deeply ingrained faith in a beneficent natural order and his native skeptical empiricism. The former notion kept a faint spark of optimism alive; the latter tendency fostered a growing pessimism. Toward the end of his life the note of pessimism seemed clearly dominant. Perhaps his study of folkways and the panorama of rising and falling cultures had led him to question more profoundly than he ever had before the straight-line abstractions of his economic studies. In 1909, the new age of misery and class conflict was for him no longer a grim possibility, but a certainty.[65] The inner logic of the political state and the drift of the mores offered neither light nor hope.

VI

However, if this pessimistic refrain gained dominance in his closing years, Sumner nevertheless during most of his life argued against state intervention from a less gloomy premise. He appears to have believed that the state, perverse though its tendencies might be, could yet be held to the path of rectitude. Nor did he make the error, common among Social Darwinists, of following out his antistatism to the point where anarchism becomes the only rational policy. Neither did he assume that the bourgeois system of property relationships was enshrined in nature and independent of state support. The state might be potentially a fountainhead of evil; but some kind of formal organization is essential to the attainment of any social good. The state must exist to enforce the rights that conduce to societal welfare. That it may and undoubtedly will ultimately destroy the rights it has created is no argument against its existence. This is merely another example of the harsh alternatives nature imposes on man in the cheerless world of Sumner's sociology.

Assuming that the state's proper function is to define and guarantee certain basic rights, Sumner faced the problem of spelling out these objectives of state authority. What were the rights, as he understood them, essential to a just society? The American democratic tradition of course supplied a set of basic concepts summed up in such catchwords as "natural rights," "liberty," and "equality," but for these notions as conventionally understood Sumner had an abiding contempt. They were "phantasms" capable of the most dangerous perversions.[66] Nevertheless, he recognized that they had, as popular symbols, accomplished some highly salutary results[67] and could be pressed into further service if carefully redefined. It became his concern, therefore, to strip the household words of democracy of their habitual meanings and to fit them out with a new character more in conformity with the objectives and values of Sumnerian conservatism.

The idea that rights are a part of man's natural heritage is sentimental nonsense. The ideal primitive condition of the philosophers never in fact existed.[68] Rights cannot be held against nature, for nature offers man nothing but the possibility of wresting a living from her if he is strong enough and clever enough to do it, and the concept of a moral claim on nature is inconsistent with the hard facts of struggle and survival. Rights are, on the contrary, created by society; they are "rules of the game of social competition which are current now and here."[69] Thus they are contingent and not absolute in any sense, being derived from "the sum of the taboos and prescriptions in the folkways."[70]

Liberty, as the term is commonly used, is similarly empty and delusory. The notion that the primitive man is free is the very opposite of the truth; the savage is a slave to nature, because, lacking tools to facilitate his struggle for subsistence, he must devote his whole life to that struggle.[71] Unbounded liberty in the sense of "doing what we please" is impossible at either end of the social scale, because nature requires that every privilege be paid for by the acceptance of some restraint. Liberty in the highest and only practicable sense is a product of civilization and thus, indirectly, of capital accumulation.[72]

As for equality, that is the most nonsensical jingle of all. There is no meaningful sense in which men can be said to be equal.[73] They differ in tastes, talents, and powers. Even equality before the law can never be perfect, and to create artificial equality in either status or physical possessions would destroy any hope for societal advance, would in fact destroy the basis on which society rests.[74]

But though rights cannot in the nature of the case possess any absolute moral validity, though they cannot be justified by reference to some mythical primitive inheritance, they can and do have a justification in utility. Some prescribed system of rights is essential to the maintenance of peace and order, which is in turn essential to community welfare. It makes no difference that such rights were originally established by force; they are nevertheless "right in the only sense we know."[75] But does this mean, as one might think at first glance, that any distribution of rights, however unequal, is as good as any other so long as order is maintained? Is an aristocracy which preëmpts privilege for the few or an ochlocracy which seizes property in the name of the majority as "moral" as the modern jural state? By no means. For Sumner is interested in discrediting the doctrine of rights only insofar as it implies a concept of good and evil based on some standard other than material utility. As quickly as it is shown then that rights are in society and not above it or antecedent to it, the proposition can be, in effect, discarded. As a sociological observation it is still of prime importance, but as an argument in the case Sumner is building up for capitalism it has served its turn.

In the second phase of the argument the issue becomes one of determining what system of rights is most serviceable to material welfare and therefore most just and deserving of state protection. And that system, Sumner tells us, is one in which rights and duties are "in equilibrium."[76] It is not always easy to see what Sumner means by this curious idea that rights and duties must balance each other in a moral political system, for it seems on the face to suggest a concept of social obligation that is foreign to the whole tendency of Sumner's thought. On analysis, however, it turns out to mean nothing of the kind. Rights and duties are said to be in equilibrium when each man receives from the social product exactly what he has earned of it and no more. A man who claims the right to a living must accept the duty of earning that living, and, conversely, the man who will not or cannot perform that duty cannot claim the right to live. He cannot claim that another man has the duty to supply him with that living, either directly or through the state, because that other man would then be accepting a duty which endowed him with no corresponding right.[77]

Such a system of rights constitutes the only meaningful definition of "civil liberty," which is "the great end for which modern states exist." [78] Moreover, Sumner is describing here something more than a mere *de facto* state of affairs: he is describing the good society. Such a system is just.[79] It is moral, because "an immoral political system is created whenever there are privileged classes — that is, classes who have arrogated to themselves rights while throwing the duties upon others." [80]

What makes this system moral, what makes it the only valid concept of justice, is its coincidence with the law of life as prescribed in the Darwinian catechism. That law decrees that every boon wrested from the earth shall be paid for by toil, either by the person who enjoys the prize or by someone else who is being forced to help support him. If the fit support only themselves under these hard conditions, then the unfit will fall by the way, and society will advance. But if the strong and capable are compelled to provide for the incompetents, then by nature's inexorable law the unfit will multiply, the accumulation of capital will be retarded, society will grow sick and decay.[81]

It will be seen that this concept of rights, strangely confused and divided though it appears, wavering between the "is" of positivism and the "ought" of moral philosophy, is infused with a coherent purpose: its ultimate objective is the elevation of the property right to a level of moral primacy. To that end, ethical concepts in general have been swept from the board, and the single norm of material welfare has been established in their place. The practical consequences of such a norm can only be the exaltation of property, of capital, of physical possessions, as ends in themselves. Then, applying the Social Darwinist assumptions, it follows that the right of the fit to keep the property their fitness has won for them is the highest good. And, since the possession of property has become the ultimate touchstone of right and wrong, all other values are relative to it and must be correspondingly redefined.

"Liberty" thus comes to mean merely such liberty as is consistent with the norm of material welfare, that is, consistent with the maintenance of the property right.[82] A very wide measure of economic freedom is therefore indicated, but other kinds of liberty are precluded if they conflict with the ruling standard. Equality is likewise transmuted into a form strange to the American democratic tradition, but congenial to the new conservatism. As one of the "cardinal principles of civil liberty," it denotes merely equality with regard to the right to have and hold.[83] It means, in short, inequality enforced by law. Even democracy is redefined in the new terminology, for a "sound and permanent" democracy is one in which equal rights are balanced by equal duties.[84] So deviations from strict social justice as Sumner defines it, departures from the ideal of economic freedom, are "undemocratic." The alchemy is complete.

VII

The importance of William Graham Sumner to the conservative tradition in America is not alone, or even chiefly, to be measured by his direct influence upon it. Substantial though his influence undoubtedly was, he shared the good work with many others, and his voice blends in the general chorus. The shaping of a national tradition is a different affair from the establishment of a "school" of doctrine, and Sumner is mainly significant, not for his original contributions to social theory, but for the special statement he gave to the naïve conservative creed. He is important as a reflection rather than as a source of popular idea patterns. He is interesting for the purposes of this study because he mirrors in special form a point of view and a metathesis of values that is characteristic of the Gilded Age.

The factor that distinguished Sumner from the other men considered in this study, and indeed from the great body of those who professed the new religion of conservatism, is, as has already been suggested, his willingness to face and accept the implications of its premises. As we have seen, even he was not altogether free from preconceptions and inconsistencies that tended to soften the hard outlines of the new dogma. He clung to a concept of morality in the face of facts which seemed to reveal that the word morality itself was meaningless. He refused to incorporate into the body of his thinking the bleakly pessimistic view of human progress that his studies implied. Nevertheless, he comes closer to consistency than most of his fellows and in his person refutes the popular notion of the professor as the murky-minded idealist who ignores hard fact. Not many, even among the tough-minded profiteers of the new era, were prepared to embrace the cheerless factual world with Sumner's fervor. In their thinking, materialism is overlaid with a stratum of sentiment, which obscures but does not alter its real character. The American temper would not, as Herbert Croly has pointed out, tolerate the Sumnerian idea that "poverty and want are an essential part of the social order";[85] and the conservative tradition tended to accept explicitly the more agreeable aspects of Sumnerism and to gloss over the rest. In Sumner himself, on the other hand, the doctrine emerges without its protective coloration and makes it possible to say: this is the new conservatism as it appears without adornments; this is the rationale, usually dimly perceived, on which the gospel of wealth must rest.

In this sense Sumner is atypical; in important ways he differs from the characteristic thinking of the age. But the difference, it should be clear, is one of degree and not of kind. In the main, Sumner moved and thought with his generation. For the age of enterprise, no less than for Sumner, the trend was away from intangible evaluations and toward materialism. The men of the age had, like Sumner, superimposed this utilitarian value system on their traditional religious dogmas, and in time, as the age progressed, the concessions to religion in this anomalous partnership became more and more perfunctory. What remained, after the spiritual base had eroded, was a frankly materialist ethic, a transference of ideas of good and right to material things. For, again like Sumner, the men of the time could not abandon the idea of an absolute morality; they could only transfigure it.

Therefore, both for Sumner and his generation, capital and the capitalist became manifestations of the highest good. The materialist ethic led inevitably to a glorification of survival value both as a standard of individual and of social merit. The capitalist system became, if not the sum, at least the apex of moral goodness; proposals to modify it by qualifying economic freedom were regarded not merely with disapproval but with horror. It is important to notice that this attitude, which beatified property and the property owner, had its basis in the ethics of material utility; but it is also important that only Sumner clearly acknowledged the fact.

Thus it can be said that both the basis of the capitalist value system and the practical effect of the system on going mores are illustrated in Sumnerism. Even more important from the viewpoint of this study, we find expressed there in clear outline the implications for democracy of this new social code. Those implications have both a negative and a positive side. In the first place, they cast a cloud over the traditional presumptions of democracy. The idea of the capitalist as social hero cannot be reconciled with the concept of popular sovereignty, which involves the premise that in one sense — and that the most important — all men are equal. In Sumnerian conservatism precisely the opposite is true; in the only sense that matters at all, men are irrevocably unequal. More especially, they are unequal in social wisdom, which is the monopoly of the businessman elite; and the inevitable conclusion is that in all practical matters the will of the people should be sharply circumscribed.

It is the restatement of democratic formulas — the "positive" side of the argument — that prescribes the limits of popular sovereignty for the new conservatism. By the only acceptable standard of right and wrong, private property is morally sacrosanct. No concept of democratic rights can justify an abridgment of economic freedom. But the idea of rights need not itself be rejected; on the contrary, it can yet serve a useful social purpose by defining the areas a democracy may not properly transgress. The idea of rights, drained of humane content, becomes concerned exclusively with the privilege of the property owner; liberty becomes economic license; and equality becomes the fiction that the village storekeeper and the Standard Oil Company enter the economic arena on equal terms. "True" democracy becomes the system of government that maintains these relationships, and the whole is overcast with a moral glow borrowed partly from religion and partly from the tradition of democracy itself. The traditional objectives of conservatism have been given a new rationale, and the process of grafting them to the main-stem of the democratic faith has begun.

four

CONSERVATISM AND CONSTITUTIONALISM:
STEPHEN J. FIELD

I

The ideas of William Graham Sumner, then, reflect a general transfiguration of the American social and political creed. This recasting of traditional thought patterns, starting from a materialist value system, produces a new definition of democracy and provides America with a new social hero in the rising entrepreneur. As the inevitable outcome of its premises, the doctrine implies a profound modification in the concept of popular sovereignty, first, because economic freedom has become the higher democratic value, and second, because when measured on a purely materialist value standard the weakness and perversity of majority rule is nakedly revealed.

This is democracy as it appears through the lenses of the new conservatism. But in tracing it thus far we have seen it only as an ideal, as a set of precepts expounded by the Polonius of Yale. It remains to be seen how Sumner's admonitions, and those of others like him, came to be embodied in the law of the land and in the conscience of the nation. The steps by which the gospel of wealth was developed follow no particular chronology. Throughout the latter half of the nineteenth century, there was a constant interaction between disquisitions of publicists and scholars, constitutional interpretations by jurists, and the attitudes of the people as a whole, so that each element affected the others and was in turn affected by them. The revolution in constitutional theory was both a cause and a symptom of the ground swell of conservative opinion in the Gilded Age.

Given the assumptions of Sumnerism and their acceptance by a significant segment of the populace, some revision in the system of constitutional limitations was imperative. In the new credo the central aim of the democratic state was the protection of the rights of property holders against unwarranted invasion. Liberty was conceived as economic liberty — in Sumner's terms, "an equilibrium of rights and duties." And since the Constitution of the United States is traditionally the palladium of freedom, since it exists to "secure the blessings of liberty," surely it would be anomalous if this great instrument left without security the only liberty really worth mentioning.

Yet, at the beginning of the postwar era, such an anomaly did in fact exist. The framers of the American Constitution were of course by no means unconcerned with the protection of property rights against governmental encroachment. As has often been shown, they were very much preoccupied with this problem. Their conception, however, of the degree and kind of economic security that ought to be provided was seen in the perspective of the 1870's to have been pitifully inadequate. They had forbidden the taking of private property for public use without compensation; they had enjoined the states from impairing the obligation of contracts; they had guaranteed the property holder a certain vague procedural protection in laws affecting him. But with these exceptions, as the Constitution stood, the rights of the man of property were subsidiary to the higher consideration of the public interest.

However, in the eyes of the new conservative there could be no higher consideration than property rights, so that the

Constitution as it stood involved a contradiction in terms. By Sumner's reasoning, the protection of economic privilege was government's one excuse for being. Obviously, then, the new conservative Jerusalem that Sumner preached must be provided with a constitutional theory in which economic freedom was regarded as ultimate.

There was another serious difficulty confronting the proponents of the new order. The reigning tradition of the Supreme Court was at variance with a dogma of popular incompetence. John Marshall was indeed very far from believing that the voice of the people is the voice of God, but by a combination of circumstances, the details of which are irrelevant here, he had been led to conclude that the *wisdom* of any legislative act is a question for the legislature's judgment. This doctrine, enunciated in *McCulloch v. Maryland*,[1] had been reiterated in a series of later decisions and, while not always scrupulously observed, was in general recognized as the accepted canon of interpretation. It was ordinarily assumed, therefore, that when the legislature possessed the constitutional authority to accomplish a given result, the Court would not interfere with its choice of means — so long as those means were "appropriate" and were not forbidden by the Constitution. In practice this meant that the legislature received the benefit of the doubt.

But the benefit of the doubt was the very thing which, on Sumner's showing, must not be conceded, particularly where property rights were involved. Such a concession imputes wisdom to the popular branch of government, to the ignorant and willful majority. It leaves the substance of constitutional freedom in the hands of the body most certain to abuse it, and places the burden of proof on those who oppose extension of governmental authority in direct violation of all reason and right. The judiciary, in following such a permissive canon of interpretation, was shirking its moral responsibility.

Nevertheless, as the case stood in about 1870, both the Constitution and the Supreme Court's traditional interpretation of it seemed ill adapted to the needs of the new conservatism. It becomes interesting to inquire then how it happens that the Court emerged in the next thirty years as the veritable stronghold of that new doctrine. For it is true that it did; in a peculiar sense the opinions of the Supreme Court became representative of conservative political theory in this period; to a remarkable degree the Constitution was reshaped to conform with the requirements of Sumnerism. To trace this evolution in broad outline and account for it is the purpose of this chapter. But it is worth while to observe at the outset that, if the actual state of constitutional precedent in 1870 seemed unfavorable to conservative objectives, there were other and compelling reasons why the situation was better than it seemed and why the Court was, in spite of appearances, well qualified for the role in which it was to be cast.

First and most obvious, the Court had been from the beginning a conservative body, conservative in the old pre-Sumnerian sense, it is true, but conservative nonetheless. And in recent years the legal profession from which the judiciary was drawn had begun to undergo a certain transformation. Tocqueville could find in 1835 that the training of lawyers tended to make them "eminently conservative and antidemocratic";[2] nevertheless, the best representatives of the American bar at that time also tended to be statesmen and philosophers. Forty years later this was hardly the case. As Brooks Adams pointed out, most successful lawyers were becoming specialists bereft of knowledge or understanding outside their narrow field. They drew their fees from corporate wealth and, by and large, their opinions as well.[3] To the native conservative bias of lawyers, the Gilded Age superadded a procapitalist prejudice that was extreme even for the nineteenth century.

Second, the Court was peculiarly suited to the purposes of the new conservatism because of the nature of its power. After years of contest, the judiciary had established its claim to review the acts of both state and federal legislatures and to disapprove them if it chose. Now, allowing for important exceptions, the main objective of capitalism in the postwar years was not to persuade the government to take action, but to prevent it from doing so. Pressure, argument, and bribery might be employed to prevent the legislative branch from passing a measure disturbing the *status quo*; even when such methods failed, the executive might be persuaded to interpose his veto. But the ultimate authority to prohibit rested with the Supreme Court. It was the focus of the negative power, and from the perspective of conservatives — chiefly concerned with negation — the Court was thus an important focal point. The conservative of the 1870's, seeking a haven for his new political dogmas, could hardly have overlooked the singular propensities of the federal judiciary.

Hence the constitutional situation as the postwar era opens was strangely contradictory. Both in the disposition of its personnel and the nature of its authority, the Supreme Court seemed predestined to become the Ark of the new conservative covenant. On the other hand, the Constitution itself and the tradition of its interpretation pointed the other way. The history of judicial review during the period is therefore in large part the story of an attempt to resolve this conflict, of a struggle between diverse instincts in the breasts of the men who composed the Supreme Court. Against their sense of social propriety and public duty was counterpoised their tendency as judges to observe precedent and the letter of the law. The lapse in time between the decision in *Munn v. Illinois*,[4] when the majority of the Court first hinted at the existence of a new concept of constitutional conservatism, and *Lochner v. New York*,[5] when the doctrine became fully articulate, is a measure of the difficulty the justices had in adapting their social convictions to their judicial scruples. They refrained from translating their political and economic prejudices directly into constitutional law because of an uneasy awareness that precedent barred the way.

But such considerations could only delay, they could not halt, the onward march of legal conservatism. The constitutional problem of the period can be recognized in perspective as one of translating Sumnerism or its equivalent into an effective system of positive law. And, one by one, the Court took the steps that brought the Constitution into line with the new social gospel and remedied the misfortune that the founding fathers had lived too soon to read either Malthus, Ricardo, or William Graham Sumner. Economic liberty, unsheltered by the original document, was granted the protection its apostles demanded. The populist-flavored notion that the legislature must be the judge of the wisdom of its own acts was sharply modified. And a new kind of social elitism was fashioned from the institution of judicial review.

II

The main vessel chosen to purvey these new judicial dogmas was the Fourteenth Amendment to the Constitution. Other clauses of the organic law reflected the conservative bias of the judges and played a significant part in the development of constitutional "laissez faire." But the Fourteenth Amendment, with particular reference to the "due process clause," was the center of conservative attention, and it is the Court's treatment of those phrases that reveals most clearly the process by which theoretical assumptions were transmuted into substantive facts.

There are several reasons why this amendment was suited to the purpose. For one thing, it had been passed so recently that judicial construction of its meaning had hardly begun, and the question of its application was thus, within certain limits, for the Court to decide. For another thing, the phrases in its opening clause were vague but extremely suggestive and admirably calculated therefore to receive what content the judges chose to pour into them. Finally, the Fourteenth Amendment was destined to become the vehicle of the new conservatism because, in spite of inherent difficulties, it offered the only peg on which the new concept of rights and liberty could conceivably be supported, unless indeed another amendment might be passed.

The phrase "due process of law," which bore the main burden of constitutional conservatism, did not of course import a substantive limitation on legislative power in its traditional interpretation.[6] On the evidence, there is in fact some question whether the phrase as it appears in the Fifth Amendment was designed to restrict the legislature at all, even in procedural matters.[7] At all events, it is fairly certain that no more than a procedural meaning could have been intended, and the opinion of Justice Curtis disposing of Chief Justice Taney's *Dred Scott* opinion on this point might have been thought to settle the issue.[8] Nevertheless, a feeling had persisted that some kinds of particularly outrageous legislation must be considered void, whether or not any explicit constitutional prohibition could be found to substantiate the feeling. This idea arose from what Morris R. Cohen has described as the American tendency "to confuse the legal and the moral," the concept of a moral standard above the law being converted into the notion that the law itself embodies that standard.[9] The confusion, illogical or not, kept alive the impression that legislatures were subject to a general substantive limit, and since in practice judges and counsel must cite something concrete, the due process clause was sometimes advanced as a candidate. The vagrant but recurring allusions to such an interpretation of the clause were enough to confuse the picture and to make it possible for the judicial process to turn the hints eventually into precedents.[10]

There are few decisions in Supreme Court history more fascinating than *Munn v. Illinois*,[11] and not the least interesting aspect of the case is its Janus-like character. On the one hand, it reveals how the minds of the judges were rooted still to old constitutional concepts; on the other hand, it foreshadows between its lines the doctrines of the future and shows how the pressures of the new day had already begun to distort judicial thinking.

The case involved the validity of a state law setting rates for grain elevators in the Chicago area. The Supreme Court was subject to an extraordinary barrage of moral, political, and economic denunciations of this "Granger" legislation, which was widely regarded as the opening wedge of the commune. With all their high emotional appeal, however, these exhortations, pouring in from counsel, from the dissenters, and from the press, were almost devoid of valid supporting legal references; when the shouting was over, it was embarrassingly clear that, no matter how immoral the Granger laws might seem, there was nothing in the United States Constitution that prohibited their enforcement. Chief Justice Waite held for the majority that the grain elevators were subject to regulation. But he did not justify his decision, as he might have, on the valid ground that no constitutional issue had been raised. He chose rather to argue that the business in question could be regulated because changing conditions had "affected it with a public interest." This curious apologetic, apparently so unnecessary, can be understood only if we recognize the paradoxical sentiments currently inspiriting the judiciary. The majority was now ready to assume, as it had not been ready three years earlier in the *Slaughter-House* decision, that the national Constitution should set some kind of substantive limitation on state laws affecting economic freedom. The moral irresponsibility of a contrary view was tacitly recognized, and the basic premise that the property right is ultimate was now fuzzily accepted.

But old-fashioned notions still barred the way to the establishment of a national system of rights on Sumner's model. The greatest difficulty was, of course, the problem of precedent. The law could be invalidated only if a substantive interpretation of the due process clause were explicitly accepted, and such an interpretation was still egregiously lacking in legal respectability. Justice Field, always a pathfinder in these matters, was willing to ignore that problem in the interests of his moral convictions; but the majority were not. Waite was obviously troubled by the arguments rained on his head. He was reluctant to declare in terms that the Constitution is irrelevant to the issue of economic freedom; neither was he ready, on the other hand, to endorse frankly an unprecedented gloss of the due process clause. He therefore clearly implied that the regulatory power is constitutionally limited and adopted the novel public-interest doctrine to explain where the limitation must be drawn. Then he showed how much farther the Court had yet to go in its political education by declaring that *when* private property is subject to regulation, the question of *how* the regulation is applied is for the legislature, not the courts, to decide. Thus he reasserted a principle already referred to — that the *wisdom* of a legislative act is outside the range of constitutional restriction.

It remained for Field to demonstrate the inconsistency of Waite's position: It is unreasonable to imply the existence of a limitation that is nonoperative. Either there is a limitation or there is not; and if there is, it should be brought into the open and applied. How can the property right be recognized as the cornerstone of morality when at the same time we acknowledge that the legislature has full discretionary authority to infringe it? Field's concept of democracy was already fully revised; that of the majority was not.

The revision could not, however, be postponed indefinitely; nor could the legal technicality that the Constitution inadequately protected property rights prevent the Court in the long run from improvising such protection. For Justice Field, the word "liberty" in the Fourteenth Amendment already meant "freedom to go where one may choose, and to act in such manner, not inconsistent with the equal rights of others, as his judgment may dictate for the promotion of his happiness; that is, to pursue such callings and avocations as may be most suitable to develop his capacities, and give to them their highest enjoyment." [12] This definition thinly veils Field's conviction that the word secures the beneficent state of economic affairs which is the first condition of social justice. That he frames the proposition more generally, that he speaks of "avocations" as well as "vocations," should not mislead us. It is economic liberty he is talking about; it is Sumnerism he is preaching. And, as is usual during this period, Field's dissent is an accurate augury of the Court's later position.

On the shadowy concept of substantive due process that appears in the *Munn* case, the Court proceeded to erect, in the next few years, an elaborate edifice of constitutional conservatism. Step by step it gave legal expression to the new social creed. In *Santa Clara County v. Southern Pacific R.R.*,[13] the judges explicitly acceded to the historically dubious argument that corporations were "persons" within the meaning of the Fourteenth Amendment. In such variant decisions as *Mugler v. Kansas* [14] and *Chicago, Milwaukee & St. Paul Ry. v. Minnesota*,[15] they undermined the doctrine that the wisdom of regulatory acts is a matter for legislative decision. In 1897, the majority formally accepted [16] a concept of "liberty" closely akin to that proffered by Justice Field, but embellished with a terminology that might have been drawn from the pages of one of Sumner's articles in *The Independent*. The curious mixture of Darwinism, Ricardianism, Malthusianism, and Spencerism which we have seen exemplified in Sumner's works had now taken over the American constitutional tradition. The further emendations that remained to be accomplished were in the nature of finishing touches which helped to make the vision of a democratic legal order rounded and complete.

In the famous case of *Lochner v. New York*,[17] these judicial achievements were classically illustrated and summarized. In this decision we can trace, either by express statement or by implication, all the major features of the dogmas which now dominated the minds of the jurists who sat on the Supreme Court. The judges had come a long way from the hesitant and fumbling immaturity of *Munn v. Illinois*.

The case involved a New York law limiting work time in the baking industry to ten hours a day. In a previous decision,[18] an act regulating hours had been upheld as applied to workers in mines and smelters, but the Court had specifically reserved the right to determine, without prejudice, whether or not such regulations in other industries would violate the due process clause. In the *Lochner* case, the majority, speaking through Justice Peckham, took advantage of that reservation to strike down the law.

The legislation, says Justice Peckham, violates freedom of contract and therefore must fall unless it can be shown that reasonable grounds exist for this specific abridgment of contractual liberty. While such abridgment may sometimes be tolerated (that is, be considered "reasonable") in the interest of the public health, the Court must examine the situation in each instance to determine whether the public health is actually involved. The length of time worked by bakers has no relevance to the nutritional quality of the bread they produce, hence the general welfare of the public is not protected by the legislation. If, on the other hand, it is argued that the protection of the health of the bakers themselves excuses the law, then it must be conceded that hours laws are permissible for all occupations, since there is nothing particularly unhealthful about the baking trade. Such a wholesale interference with contractual freedom is unthinkable; therefore, the law is invalid.

All our familiar friends of contemporary social theory are here in thin disguise. In the first place, it should be noted that the old presumption of legislative wisdom has been formally discarded. This conclusion was ultimately unavoidable and was contained by inference in the Court's original assumption that economic liberty is the holy of holies in a just constitutional system. By degrees, since the 1870's, this basic Sumnerian premise had assumed the character of an axiomatic truth; and from that premise the law had proceeded to the clearly implied conclusion. The deep distrust of legislative majorities which was inherent in the conservative ethic had become a principle of American constitutional law.

And in thus whittling away the legislative prerogative, the Court had revealed another equally important consequence of its current social philosophy. The modern doctrines divided men into the "classes" and the "masses," asserting that inequality is the rule of life and that only the elect few are capable of making the decisions that control society. The highest pinnacle of honor and trust was reserved, of course, in Sumner's system, for the businessman, who had earned his title to nobility by success in the economic arena. But the justices would have been less than human had they not assimilated some of his glory to their own august personages. The essential point, given the original antipopulist bias, is that there are the few with merit and the many without. The great importance of the *Lochner* decision in American constitutional history is that the Court there explicitly assumed the dispensing power and asserted that, whereas legislators are incompetent to decide ultimate questions of social policy, the courts are not. Justice Peckham not only claimed the right to judge whether the legislature had acted wisely in choosing to regulate economic relationships; he also refused to be bound by any rule in making that judgment, thus establishing the judiciary as a censorial elite.

Finally, the hallowed democratic watchwords such as "liberty" and "equality" were given their full-fledged modern gloss in Justice Peckham's opinion. Both words now implied, in the Court's philosophy as in Sumner's, an unadorned endorsement of the strong and wealthy at the expense of the weak and poor. The "liberty" enshrined in the Constitution now can be recognized as a euphemism for entrepreneurial privilege. And the notion of "equality," for constitutional purposes, had become the amiable fiction that the employer and the unorganized worker stand as equals at the bargaining table. The originally humanistic doctrines of liberal democracy had been refashioned as pillars of the new conservatism.

III

We have now seen in the writings of William Graham Sumner the development of the premises that form the bedrock of postwar conservative ideology and have noticed that the Supreme Court of the nineteenth century translated those precepts into positive legal conventions. A really thorough study of how this constitutional legerdemain was accomplished might fill several volumes, for it would involve, among other things, a detailed consideration of contemporary legal materials and a vast enterprise in the field of judicial biography. The modest pretensions of this essay will be fulfilled, however, by observing how the currents of conservative doctrine affected the life and thought of one great legal figure and through him were transformed into tenets of American constitutional law. His story will supply at least an inkling of the subtle and complicated process that shaped the American mind and the American legal system in the Gilded Age.

I have suggested that judicial acceptance of the Sumnerian ideology was inevitable from the first, because the people of America and the judges with them had embraced, more or less wholeheartedly, the major postulates of the conservative creed. But the matter is not so simple as this unqualified statement of it might suggest. Popular acceptance would have been less likely and constitutional expression of the ideal would have been nearly impossible if the justices had copied the Sumnerian model precisely as it came from his hand. Sumner's version of the conservative gospel was both too explicit and too uncompromising. In the constitutional structure that the judiciary was erecting some play had to be allowed to the joints if the machine was to work.[19] Expediency requires concessions that Sumner in his academic Erewhon would never allow. Moreover, even as an ideal, Sumnerism had characteristics that made it generally unpalatable in its undiluted form. Neither the people nor the jurists could quite swallow the social philosophy of *What Social Classes Owe to Each Other* unless its real nature was partially disguised, its harsh edges somewhat softened. The age was prepared to adopt a materialist standard of right, but it was not prepared to admit that it had done so. It was prepared to subordinate humanitarianism to business needs, but it was reluctant to spell out the subordination frankly and explicitly.

Another difficulty was that Sumner's attack on democracy was too outspoken for general consumption. He had no comfortable notion that the traditions of American democracy supported his conservative cause; his redefinition of such terms as democracy, liberty, rights, and equality was a more or less candid proposal that received interpretations of these catchwords should be abandoned. His contempt for traditional democratic symbolism was unconcealed, nor can a reader avoid the inference that it is a new world he envisions rather than a continuation of the old. And while public opinion was content to see the substance of the democratic myth revamped, the shadow had to be retained. Both the moral instincts of Americans and their political traditions required that natural law be invoked to support any new ideology, that a semblance of continuity with the American past be scrupulously preserved.

Finally, Sumner's social theory was too much infused with pessimism to suit the temper of the Century of Progress. He foresaw a chronically ailing social order, a future that offered little to look forward to and much to dread. This joyless prognosis was in sharp contrast to a national spirit confident of the "automatic ascent of American things to unprecedented magnificences." [20]

To make the doctrine acceptable, then, the hard outlines of the conservative credo as Sumner stated it must be concealed; the dogmas must be more ambiguously stated. The pitiless implications of Social Darwinism must be ignored or passed over quickly; any hint of a break with the democratic past must be adjured; the Sumnerian gloom must be brightened with a touch of optimism. For only if these revisions were incorporated could conservatism really prevail. It could not ignore the prevailing climate; it could not run athwart established ideas of the "American way," but rather must take them over and use them for its own. And this revisionist compulsion was no less great for the judicial fraternity than for the people as a whole.

From the viewpoint of one concerned with the nature of this process of alteration and acceptance, a consideration of Stephen J. Field (1816–1899) is singularly appropriate. His thirty-four years on the bench of the Supreme Court, from 1863 to 1897, almost exactly correspond with the growing period of the conservative ideology: when he retired, conservatism had matured both as a philosophy and as a constitutional dogma. Partly with his help it had assumed most of the lineaments that distinguish it from unadulterated Sumnerism — the semireligious moral aroma, the identification with historic democracy, the sanction of natural law. Field did not himself contrive this conservative triumph, of course, nor can we safely impute to him much direct influence on the mind of the nation. But he did profoundly influence the character of American law, and his judicial opinions provide an excellent illustration of conservatism in transition; they show how it was possible for a brutally materialist ethic to disguise itself as democracy. We can see, in the relationship of Field to the legal fraternity, something of the way in which ideas are transmitted from a powerful advocate to an audience that has already accepted the essential postulates of his case. For Field was to the Court what the great crowd of conservative publicists was to the country at large — a gadfly, an instructor, and a prophet.

Like Sumner, Field was brought up in New England and was exposed in his youth to the religious dogmas that were the contemporary survivals of Puritanism.[21] His father occupied the pulpit in Stockbridge, Massachusetts, from which the great Puritan divine, Jonathan Edwards, had once hurled his rhetorical thunderbolts. On the authority of Stephen's brother, Henry, their father was Edwards' follower in more senses than one. It was no modernized gospel that the elder Field preached, no sugar-coated doctrine of redemption from God's wrath through divine mercy. God was for him as for Edwards a vessel of wrath, and his world was a world of absolutes with no subtle shadings between right and wrong, between good and evil. The truth was tangible, certain, unquestionable, and eternal, and in the struggle against error there could be no compromise.

Thrice each Sunday Stephen and his brothers listened to sermons in which ideas such as these were set forth, a world such as this pictured. Throughout the week on a more informal basis, they were trained by precept and example in the standards of Christian conduct as their father and mother understood them. When Stephen grew up and left Stockbridge, he put away as Sumner did the outer shell of religious orthodoxy, but it is hardly likely that such conditioning left him unaffected. Through all his life Field's thinking was of a character in which the influence of his Puritan upbringing can be faithfully traced. The dividing line between good and evil remained always clear and sharp in his mind; the relationship between them was fixed: it was an "eternal verity." Those who proposed action that violated this clear dichotomy were not merely wrong, they were outrageously wrong; they were sinners. A profoundly moral tone pervaded many of his judicial utterances; legal issues were stated in ethical terms; "right" rather than precedent tended to be the guiding consideration. And conjoined to this preoccupation with normative questions was a remarkable sense of certainty concerning the answers. Field did not believe something to be right — he knew it to be; and the self-righteousness thereby generated was a dominant feature of his juridical personality.

It is interesting to observe in later years the position occupied by the deity in the Fieldian cosmology. Sumner, it will be remembered, looked back in the drawer to which he had consigned his religious beliefs and found nothing there at all. This adoption of an agnostic view was the inevitable outcome of the baldly empirical position he had assumed in his pursuit of scientific verity. The concept of a living God was obviously at variance with his principles, and Sumner was never consciously inconsistent. However, Field as a jurist was under no such obligation to maintain a consistent attitude on metaphysical issues. He could reject the God of organized religion and scriptural authority, yet retain him as a sort of personal deity whose prescriptions on social matters curiously and faithfully confirmed those advanced by Judge Field. The coöperation of this sympathetic Omnipotence could thus be invoked in support of any given theory of right or justice whether or not chapter and verse could be cited to verify the divine intent.

It is these survivals of Field's religious training, rather than an individualist bias arising out of "the Puritan conception of consociation," [22] which seem to have been most decisive in the formation of his thought and character. Insofar as Protestantism supports an individualist view, Field undoubtedly absorbed it, but in his early years as a lawyer and judge that individualism "was tempered by a calm, social point of view." [23] It was only later, when other influences had set his thinking in a new frame of reference, that Field, in common with the rest of the nation, turned the tradition of the free individual into a full-blown theory of economic "laissez faire." The same generalization applies too, I think, to the Puritan conception of the chosen few. This idea could be translated readily enough into the doctrine that society must submit to the rule of an elite composed of businessmen and judges; but it was not so translated for Field until his conservatism had matured.

It is not suggested that the concepts of the free individual and of a moral aristocracy were negligible elements in Field's early thought, but rather that the precise content of these notions was subject to variation as other idea patterns took form. They did not in themselves saddle his thinking with a prejudice in favor of untrammeled business enterprise. His understanding of the meaning and implications of individualism changed with the times. It may be only a step, as Weber and Tawney have made clear, from the Protestant to the capitalist ethic; but there is a gap between them; the step must be taken.

On the other hand, Field's belief that there *were* eternal verities, that they were absolute and unshaded, and that he was endowed with special insight into their nature — this belief never wavered. This assurance is the constant factor in his thought, the quality that distinguishes him from many of his fellow conservatives who embraced their convictions more tentatively. Puritanism and the American individualist tradition prepared his mind for the capitalist ideology, but this was more or less true of his whole generation. Field's conservatism was special, not because of the content of his views, not because his idea of what is good or right differed from the ideas of his contemporaries, but because he used such terms as his father would have used them, as moral absolutes from which there could be no appeal. And it is this dogmatism about the *nature* of truth, which he may well have drawn from the rigorous Calvinism of his childhood, that so admirably equipped him to play a part in the conservative restatement of democracy.

Similar observations are suggested by Field's educational experience, at Williams College, which he entered at the age of sixteen, and in his brother's law office, where he prepared himself for admission to the bar. At Williams, he encountered Mark Hopkins, and while there is no direct evidence that Hopkins influenced him profoundly, more than one student of Field has been led to infer such an influence from a comparison of their ideas.[24] Hopkins did argue in his *Lectures on Moral Science*[25] that government exists to secure the rights of the individual and that those rights are inalienable, even by contract. He also insisted that the desire to accumulate property serves a beneficent social purpose. It is not unlikely that in later life, as he groped for a formulation of his concepts of constitutional morality, Justice Field harked back to the homiletics of his great teacher. But such ideas were abroad everywhere in the nineteenth century, and Field might have borrowed the rationale that framed his defense of capitalism from dozens of other sources. On the other hand, if Hopkins' substantive ideas were commonplace, the manner in which he expounded them was not. He was convinced that the answers to human problems could be deduced systematically and intelligibly from a few simple theorems, and he conducted his pupils along this path of enlightenment with masterly skill. The mind of young Field, already most at home in a world of black and white, must have found the specious certitude of this method most congenial. It seems likely that Mark Hopkins transmitted to the future jurist a habit of mind rather than a specific doctrinal persuasion.

From 1838 to 1841 Field studied law, first with his brother, David Dudley Field, then with John Van Buren, later Attorney General of New York. After admission to the bar, he practiced with his brother in New York until 1848. There is much about the practice and study of law in that time and context that must have confirmed his mental predispositions. The law was commonly supposed at that time to proceed from a few "timeless principles" perceptible to man, as James Wilson said, "in a manner more analogous to the perceptions of sense than to the conclusions of reasoning." [26] From these simple and self-evident starting points, the judges drew the threads of logic to an inevitable conclusion. Moreover, throughout the time of the Field brothers' partnership, David Dudley was engaged in his struggle to codify the law of New York, and it seems reasonable to believe that Stephen could not have gone untouched by his elder's enthusiasm. The idea of a code implies, even in its sophisticated form, the possibility of discovering constant principles and applying them by logical process to human situations — a notion already so familiar to Field as to be taken as an article of faith.

Field left David Dudley's firm in 1848 and, after a year in Europe, took ship for California to try his fortunes in the gold rush. He plunged into that anarchic world with zest, apparently not a whit daunted by its remarkable contrast to the moral environment of Stockbridge and Williamstown, but finding in it both a stimulus and the promise of great opportunities for an enterprising young attorney. The details of his life there need not delay us, but its general outlines are important to an understanding of the man. Leaving San Francisco where he had disembarked, he took part in founding the town of Marysville, became its first alcalde, and began a series of real-estate speculations which netted substantial returns. As a magistrate he administered affairs, according to his own account, with great success and doled out justice, including public floggings, to the satisfaction of all. He was elected to the new state Legislature in 1850, served one term, and was defeated in an effort to gain a seat in the California Senate. He then devoted himself for several years to the practice of law and to participation in a number of quarrels in which he displayed a violent temper, a considerable degree of vindictiveness, and — if we can accept the authority of his own *Reminiscences* — a good deal of cool courage. Whether he played the rather heroic part in these fracases that he assigns to himself or that of the abject coward some of his enemies described is of no great importance. The significant point is that Field thought of himself as a man's man in a man's world, took to carrying a bowie knife and revolver, and in general subscribed to the code of self-reliance that frontier conditions ordained. He achieved substantial success as a practicing attorney, but the siren call of politics was then, as always, irresistibly sweet to him, and in 1857 he was elected to the state Supreme Court.

It is difficult to generalize about the state of mind engendered by frontier existence. Later consideration has at least cast some doubt on the easy assumption of earlier historians that the pioneer spirit is favorable to the growth of genuine democratic ideals. Perhaps it is safest to say that the temperament developed under frontier conditions will be determined largely by predispositions, whether it is a people or an individual we are talking about. And certainly, in the case of an individual, it will make a difference if his experience has resulted in personal success or in failure.

Field was a success on the frontier. Eight years after his arrival in California, he had been chosen for one of the state's highest public offices. In the year preceding his elevation to the bench, he had earned forty-two thousand dollars. This rapid rise contrasted sharply with his relatively undistinguished career in New York under the shadow of his eminent brother, and it must have seemed to the young attorney that he had at length come into his own. We know from the *Reminiscences* that he regarded his years in California as the most stimulating of his life; it was the state of his adoption rather than of his nativity that he thought of as home. It seems justifiable to infer that the lessons learned, the standards ingrained under such conditions, played a decisive part in the man's intellectual development. This is all the more true, of course, since his frontier experience could so easily be interpreted as confirming assumptions he was already disposed to make about himself and the world around him.

Two assumptions appear to have dominated Field's mental scheme at the time he came to California. In the first place, he assumed that he himself was a superior being, a leader among men. The genealogy of such an idea is not hard to find in the Calvinistic doctrines of his father's church; the notion must have been twice enforced by a growing consciousness of how remarkable his family was, how easily his brothers,

Cyrus and David Dudley, had reached commanding positions in the world of affairs. Any doubts he may have had about his own title to such distinction must have been dispelled by the personal success he quickly achieved, starting almost from scratch, in fighting his way up in the contentious West. By frontier standards, indeed by the standard of the time anywhere, he had every reason to feel satisfied with himself; there is every reason to believe that he did.

In the second place, as I have said, Field's whole training had been such as to inculcate a view of the nature of truth and right that was peculiarly absolutist. There may be some argument about whether life under frontier conditions tends independently to foster such a conviction; for the subtle-minded it may well produce an opposite result. But the frontier is not friendly to subtleties. Its moral problems are not abstract but intensely practical; they cannot be left to casuists who complicate and obscure them, for the very existence of the social order requires that they be stated dogmatically and enforced without exception. The model frontiersman is Owen Wister's Virginian, whose whole concept of right and duty is derived from a few simple postulates firmly maintained against all the promptings of sentiment. Field found little in the California of gold-rush days to disturb his original moral outlook; he must have found much to support it.

But if from most points of view it may be inferred that life on the frontier provided Field merely with a confirmation of his own presumptions, in at least one important respect it may have affected him more radically. The salient characteristic of American thought in postwar years, the quality that prepared the way for the ideological triumph of conservatism, was an essentially materialist bias; and it is not unlikely that Field was forearmed to accept such a value system by his California experience. A far richer imagination than Field's was marred by a similar set of early impressions. Mark Twain's early ideal, the frontier rowdy, was replaced by the entrepreneur and the inventor. "These types became his creators: they alone were the people who furnished life with an amplitude of meaning, and because of their works, the Nineteenth Century was the 'plainest and sturdiest and infinitely greatest and worthiest of all the centuries the world has seen.' " [27] What the frontier could do to Mark Twain it could do to Field. He too must have absorbed its materialist value standard, for he too later accepted the businessman as the social hero, economic progress as the badge of civilization. Neither in Mark Twain nor in Field was the transition from pioneer ideals to those of capitalism immediate; the industrial day itself had to dawn to produce the mutation. But in the minds of both the path was cleared for idealization of material ends.

In these ways the ideas of Field were firmly set by 1857 when his judicial career began. His estimate of himself, an exalted one, had been endorsed by his experience. A dogmatic view of right was vindicated by all his training, and each successive development in his career drove deeper the conviction that he was especially well equipped for the role of Moses. His personal ideal, the man of forthright action, had been exemplified for him in the rugged frontiersman and in his own vision of himself. Now such ideas as these, it should be noted, are clues to Field's personality rather than to the substantive content of his thought. They do not in themselves explain why Field so ardently championed the capitalist ideology in later years. But they do explain why the shift in his thinking when it did come was so rapidly consummated; they explain why, having accepted the new gospel, he would tolerate no compromise with its main principles; they explain the high moral tone that always infused his pronouncements on the subject; and they help to explain his commanding position in any history of the Supreme Court.

It has been necessary to make this distinction between the

elements in Field's thought that were present from the first and his more variable convictions in order to see his intellectual development in its proper perspective in relation to the contemporary climate of opinion. For during his California days, as Professor Swisher has shown, Field was not the doctrinaire conservative that he was in a later period. His legislative record and his opinions from the bench bespeak, on the contrary, a moderate social philosophy and a genuine concern for the plight of the poor and oppressed. Evidently, the hard mold of the capitalist ethic had yet to take form in his mind.

Field's accomplishments during his single term in the California Legislature are remarkable both in their range and quantity. He is said to have drafted the law regulating mining claims which became the model for other states and for Congress itself. He drew up and secured the adoption of codes of civil and criminal procedure on the order of those his brother had formulated for the state of New York, but remodeled to suit California conditions. He found time to repay with interest an affront he had received from Judge Turner, a Marysville enemy. Field's "Bill concerning the Judiciary of the State" gerrymandered Turner out of his district and sent him to preside over court in a remote wilderness. Most important of all from the viewpoint of this study, however, is the legislation Field sponsored on behalf of debtors. His Civil Practise Act contained a provision granting substantial exemptions from forced sale, exemptions more generous than those afforded by the laws of most other states. By his own account, he supported a Homestead Exemption Act that granted exemptions up to $5000, instead of the $3000 maximum some of the other legislators had proposed.[28]

Standing in even sharper contrast to his judicial attitude of later years is his dissenting opinion in *Ex parte Newman*.[29] This case, decided in 1858 during his first term on the California Supreme Court, involved a state law requiring places of business to close their doors on Sundays. The legislation was challenged on the ground that, by designating Sunday as a compulsory day of rest, it discriminated in favor of the Christian religion and thus violated the state constitution; and that, by prohibiting the pursuit of a lawful occupation, it contravened the constitutional provision which secured the inalienable right of "acquiring, possessing, and protecting property." The court majority invalidated the law on these grounds.

Justice Field dissented. The Legislature, he said, has merely "given the sanction of law to a rule of conduct which the entire civilized world recognizes as essential to the physical and moral well being of society. . . One day in seven is the rule, founded on experience and sustained by science. . . This fact has not escaped the observation of men of science, and distinguished philosophers have not hesitated to pronounce the rule founded upon a law of our race." The Legislature has the right to pass laws for the preservation of health and morals, "and if it is of the opinion that periodical cessation from labor will tend to both, and thinks proper to carry its opinion into statutory enactment, there is no power, outside of its constituents which can sit in judgment on its action. It is not for the judiciary to assume a wisdom which it denies to the legislature, and exercise a supervision over the discretion of the latter. It is not the province of the judiciary to pass upon the wisdom and policy of legislation; and when it does so, it usurps a power never conferred by the constitution.

"It is no answer to the requirements of the statute to say that mankind will seek cessation from labor by the natural influences of self-preservation. The position assumes that all men are independent and at liberty to work whenever they choose. Whether this be true or not in theory, it is false in fact; it is contradicted by every day's experience. . . The law steps in to restrain the power of capital. . . Authority for the enactment I find in the great object of all government, which is protection. Labor is a necessity imposed by the condition of our race, and to protect labor is the highest office of our laws." [30]

This opinion, so startling from the pen of one of the century's arch-conservatives, so unequivocally expressing an attitude of humanity and legislative tolerance, stands squarely across the path of any student who seeks to understand Field's mental processes. Professor Swisher sees it as a "cross thread," a temporary deviation from the main direction of his thinking, explainable only in the sense that it proves Field's development did not follow a direct and simple line from beginning to end. The biographer also points out, rightly of course, that it is risky to build too much on the general principles enunciated by a judge who is arguing a cause; for judges, as for less lordly men, the principle is sometimes tailored to fit the result.

Even when these points are taken into account, however, the feeling remains that more must be said. The views expressed in the opinion are too heretical to be excused lightly. Three cardinal tenets of the future conservative creed are directly and explicitly forsworn. The legislature's authority to judge the wisdom of its own acts is reasserted, and *a fortiori* the doctrine of judicial control is renounced. The problem of equality between labor and capital is viewed realistically and without the sophistic gloss we can later observe in such decisions as *Lochner v. New York*. Finally, the concept of a social system organized to promote the welfare of the businessman by leaving him alone is exchanged for a doctrine which would restrain capital in the interests of justice and humanity. These are ideas which could lift Field, twenty years later, to the summits of righteous indignation when he encountered them in the arguments of counsel or the opinions of his fellow members on the Supreme Court of the United States; yet he sets them down here with all the appearance of earnest conviction. It need not be believed that, even in 1858, he accepted these notions quite so wholeheartedly as the terms he used might suggest. But it is almost impossible to believe, on the other hand, that he could have written so if the main outlines of the capitalist ethic were already firmly set in his mind. It must be concluded, I think, that the social outlook of Field in the 1850's was significantly at variance with his later credo; that neither Puritanism, nor his education, nor his frontier experiences were directly responsible for the substantive ideas he was to express in the *Slaughter-House Cases*; and that something happened during the intervening years to alter the character of his social premises.

Field seems to have been in fact, at this stage of his development, a conservative of a type that gradually became almost extinct in the decades following the Civil War. A high respect for the sanctity of property rights did not carry with it the assumption that the owner of the property could do no wrong or that a government could rightfully disregard the welfare of other elements in its population in order to protect capital. A belief in the ideal of limited constitutional government did not necessarily imply that the functions of the legislature should be usurped by the judiciary. The idea was rather to balance the just claims of conflicting groups and of separate branches of government, and thereby to maintain a social and moral equilibrium. In this sense Field was closer at the time to the conservatism of John Adams than to that of William Graham Sumner. The constants in his character — an absolutist view of right and a consciousness of personal superiority — shine through the phrases of this opinion: note the discovery of a "law of our race" in the habit of Sabbath observance; note the self-assured, positive tone. But the idea that the property right is fundamental and inalienable has not yet been crystallized into the dogma that it is all-absorbing. And the feeling of superiority leads him to assume a protective attitude toward the weak rather than to rally the judiciary in support of the strong.

Thirteen years later, as a justice of the national Supreme Court, Field's social orientation seems to have shifted. The tone of his dissent in the *Legal Tender Cases* [31] is not distinguishable from the positive self-assurance of *Ex parte Newman*. But the substance of his complaint is quite different. Henceforward he is the capitalist doctrinarian incarnate with whom posterity is best acquainted. Patently something has happened to modify his social philosophy in the interim; if the line of continuity in his thought has not been broken, at least it has sharply swerved.

The nature of the influences that played upon his mind from 1858 to 1871 and combined to produce this defection from his earlier position cannot be certainly determined, and any analysis of them must proceed by inference. But the inferences must be drawn. For the changes in Field's thought are comparable to the transition in the mind of his age, and they must be explained in order to understand not only Field but America.

The great omnipresence during this pivotal decade in American thought was, of course, the Civil War and its aftermath. In that crucible were produced not merely a new South but a new nation. Said Henry Adams, referring to his return to American soil in 1868: "Had they been Tyrian traders of the year B.C. 1000, landing from a galley fresh from Gibraltar, they could hardly have been stranger on the shore of a world, so changed from what it had been ten years before." [32] The cataclysm had compressed a profound economic upheaval into a few short years; it had introduced almost overnight the vast complexities of an industrial society; it had bred up a new race of entrepreneurs who acknowledged no morality but pecuniary success. The nation had been brought to the point of ethical exhaustion. "The old idealism had been burnt away, the hopes of the patriot fathers, the youthful and generous dreams of the early republic. The war, with its fearful tension, draining the national vitality, had left the mind of the people morally flabby." [33] Croce's words applied to Europe describe post-bellum America even more nicely: "When the great political battles were over, the new generations, and even the old patriots and combatants, devoted themselves to business; and competition and struggle for markets, in their turn, helped to suggest the primacy of energy, force, practical capacity, over ethical and national motives. The great economic prosperity that was supposed to supply new and plentiful gifts to the work of human ideality seemed, on the contrary, rather to suffocate it." [34]

The effect of the war, as this statement suggests, was not only to waste away the old democratic values of American life, but to raise up new gods and new ideals in their vacated places. The new capitalism required a gospel of assertion as well as of negation; its position would not be secure if it rested only on moral indifference: it needed positive support, discipleship. And one of its early converts was Stephen Field. He, like most of his generation, was emotionally submerged in the fray, participated in the spiritual convulsion that it generated, was exposed to the ideological revolution that followed. He could not have remained unaffected by this violent upheaval in economic conditions and social ideals. He felt the impulsion of the new standards and responded to them, putting aside, as many others did, his pre-Sumter frame of reference. There were those in Field's generation who could not make the adjustment so readily. The younger men who were bred to the modern *Zeitgeist* absorbed it as a matter of course; but others, like the Bostonian father in *The Rise of Silas Lapham*, were less introceptive, and they felt that the age was passing them by. But Field's roots were not so deep in the old tradition; the years in the West had helped to keep him young, so that when the new Truth dawned, he could welcome it unhesitatingly.

And his training had prepared him to accept the new creed without cavil or reservation. Having embraced its postulates, by a habit of mind which had become a law of his nature he pressed them to extremes. Instinctively he leaped to conclusions which his fellows approached less resolutely and began thundering the axioms of the faith as if they had been established since the fall of Adam. Then indeed, but only then, the ideal of the free individual became identified in his mind with economic liberty; right became capitalist privilege; his elitist notions led him to elevate both himself as a judge and the businessman as a social hero to the ranks of a ruling squirearchy. And because of his innate dogmatism, because of his confidence in his own perspicacity, he was able to lead his brother justices who, driven by the same impulses, were less quick to respond.

Other factors besides the moral impact of the war and its sequel undoubtedly help to account for the development in Field's social tenets. His political ambitions became more and more decisive in his pattern of motivations, as we shall later see. The friendship of men like Stanford and Huntington probably flattered his vanity and tempted him to identify himself — also a leader and an empire-builder in another realm of activity — with them and their cause. But political motives were dominant in his decisions only when no conflict with important property rights was involved, and the railroad kings could not have impressed him so emphatically unless he had already in large part adopted their world as his own. That he had done so is hardly surprising. For a man of his background, who had to believe in something but lacked the spirit of the reformist or the intellectual resources to transcend his environment, there was very little choice. So Stephen Field learned to believe in capital and capitalists and to remake his social ideals on their models. And the political philosophy that underlies his constitutional opinions, for all its interesting variations on the Sumnerian pattern, is unmistakably cut from the same bolt of cloth. The variations help, as I have said, to make the product salable, but they should not be allowed to conceal the basic homogeneity in the ideas of the two men.

five

JUDICIAL CONSERVATISM AND
THE RIGHTS OF MAN

I

In Field's Supreme Court opinions involving issues of more than technical significance, surely few words occur more often, and none is more important, than "rights." The term seems to echo with a sort of magic for him; he is confident it will cut any knot of legal complexity, and he uses it repeatedly for that purpose. It had always had a certain magical quality for Americans generally, for it was imbedded deep in their political presumptions by way of Sidney, Locke, and Milton, in their legal tradition through Coke and Blackstone, and enshrined in the Declaration for all time. Furthermore, popular awareness of the concept of rights had received a terrific impetus in the prewar controversy over slavery, and the word was still ringing in the ears of the nation. It was therefore both natural and providential that Field should seize upon the term and make it the fulcrum of his legal and political theory.

The way in which he would use such a concept — as distinct from the content he would give it — had been determined years before when his notions of morality first took root. For Field, rights could only be natural, inalienable, immutable. To regard them otherwise would be to concede that truth is inconstant, that right and wrong may sometimes be hard to distinguish. Field would have found such an idea nearly incomprehensible. He endowed his concept of rights with the authority of a command from God; he identified it with the American natural-law tradition; and he claimed for it all the prestige that had accrued during the preceding two centuries to the ideal of democracy.

As in our intercourse with our fellow men certain principles of morality are assumed to exist, without which society would be impossible, so certain inherent rights lie at the foundation of all action, and upon a recognition of them alone can free institutions be maintained. These inherent rights have never been more happily expressed than in the Declaration of Independence, that new evangel of liberty to the people: "We hold these truths to be self-evident" — that is, so plain that their truth is recognized upon their mere statement — "that all men are endowed" — not by edicts of emperors or decrees of parliament, or acts of Congress, but "by their Creator with certain inalienable rights" — that is, rights which cannot be bartered away, or given away, or taken away except in punishment of crime — "and that among these are life, liberty, and the pursuit of happiness, and to secure these" — not grant them but secure them — "governments are instituted among men, deriving their just powers from the consent of the governed." [1]

Thus Field spoke in exalted terms of the right of butchers in New Orleans to slaughter their cattle as they pleased. The noble sentiments as well as the majestic words were those familiar to generations of Americans for whom they had an eternally beguiling ring. This is the kind of language they would expect to hear from one who stated the principles of American constitutionalism.

Similarly no one, except possibly a lawyer, was likely to be surprised when, in *Cummings v. Missouri*,[2] Field invalidated a state test oath on the grounds that it abridged rights secured by "the theory upon which our political institutions rest." [3] The requirement, he said, subverts "the presumption of innocence, and alters the rules of evidence, which heretofore, under the universally recognized principles of the common law, have been supposed to be fundamental and unchangeable." [4] Since the state constitutions had adopted the common law only until the legislatures might choose to change it, and since the Fourteenth Amendment was not yet available as an instrument of judicial lawmaking, this was bad legal history, but it illustrates the readiness with which Field bestowed the quality of universality on principles he deemed to be just. The same note is struck in *Beckwith v. Bean* [5] involving the military arrest and imprisonment of a private citizen in Vermont. Field insisted that the rights of the petitioner had been arbitrarily invaded. "It is only the extraordinary claim made by the counsel of the government in this case which justifies any argument in support of principles so fundamental and heretofore so universally recognized. It may be necessary at times with respect to them, as it is necessary with respect to admitted principles of morality, to re-state them in order to rescue them from the forgetfulness caused by their universal admission." [6]

God is frequently called to the support of Field's principles in order to ensure them the last full measure of dignity. "The only loyalty which I can admit consists in obedience to the Constitution and laws made in pursuance of it," he said in the *Legal Tender Cases*. [7] "It is only by obedience that affection and reverence can be shown to a superior having a right to command. So thought our great Master when he said to his disciples: 'If ye love me, keep my commandments.'" It is the Creator who grants rights and forbids any government to transgress them. They are, like the Decalogue itself, not mere arrangements prescribed by custom (as Sumner would have argued) but ethical imperatives whose abstract validity is unaffected by shifts in popular inclination. To attack them is to attack Justice.

In using this vocabulary of rights, natural and God-given, Field was but joining a long procession of American statesmen and legalists, not to speak of preachers, who had used the language in various ways to justify various points of view. Like them, he spoke in abstractions because, characteristically, he saw the issues not as purely legal or policy questions, but as problems of moral right. The natural-law philosophy and its corollary of natural rights had been subjected to a heavy barrage of criticism in recent years, mostly on the positivist ground that it was historical nonsense and obscured the true relationship between society and the individual. "When was it enacted?" said Thomas Cooper. "By Whom? or by what power has it been sanctioned?" [8] For Sumner, devotion to such an ideal was simply fatuous; it was a superstition surviving to befuddle men's minds in a matter-of-fact world. Yet here is this "phantasm," as Sumner would have called it, being invoked in the name of the very social system Sumner championed. And it seems, at first glance, strangely out of place in that system, whose God is the balance sheet, whose gospel is realism, whose saints are the entrepreneurs. The incongruity, however, has a method about it, and the contradiction is more apparent than real. For what Sumner failed to see was that the capitalist ideal he defended must somehow be incorporated in the American democratic myth and that his own religion of frank empiricism was completely unsuitable to accomplish that end. And what those who mistake Justice Field's philosophy for extramundane fail to see is that the real nature of a political philosophy is determined, not by the symbols it employs, but by the objectives it seeks, by the substantive content its terms are given.

What is the content then of the term "rights" as Field employs it? To answer this key question we must follow the jurist through a number of decisions in which he made the concept articulate, bearing in mind that from first to last he was, either expressly or by clear implication, equating his prescripts with the traditions of American democracy.

A very friendly biographer has described Field's philosophy of rights as follows:

> The upholding and enforcement as a matter of special moment, of all those particular restrictions upon the governmental action, both of the United States and of the several states, contained in the original Constitution and in the amendments, which are intended directly to protect the private rights of life, liberty, and property, and, in fact, that entire body of private rights which constitute "civil liberty." [9]

At first glance this would appear to be a reasonably accurate statement of Field's attitude. Let us see how analysis bears it out.

In the *Milligan* case,[10] Field was one of the five members of the Court who declared that neither the President nor the Congress had authority to establish military commissions to try civilians outside the actual war zone while civil courts were open and functioning. This was, as Field later said, a decision "in favor of the liberty of the citizen." [11] A year later, he wrote the majority decisions in the famous Test Oath cases.[12] He labored hard in the *Cummings* decision to establish the proposition that the oath requirements involved punishment for past conduct and were hence invalid under the *ex post facto* and bill of attainder provisions of the Constitution. The "theory upon which our political institutions rest" prescribes that "in the pursuit of happiness all avocations, all honors, all positions, are alike open to everyone." [13] A law which qualifies those privileges must be regarded as inflicting punishment. In the *Beckwith* case, Field was willing to go farther than the Court majority in limiting an army provost-marshal's discretion to subvert the ordinary procedural guarantees. The plaintiff had been held without trial for several months under suspicion that he had helped two substitutes desert the Union Army. He brought action for damages against the military officials who had imprisoned him and was awarded $15,000. On appeal, the Supreme Court held that evidence of the plaintiff's probable guilt was admissible as mitigation for damages; a new trial was ordered, although the officers were scolded for detaining the prisoner unduly. Whether he was guilty or innocent, declared Field in dissent, this was "a gross outrage upon [his] rights. . . I know not why (under the Court's construction) the violence of mobs, excited against guilty or suspected parties, may not find extenuation. Let such a doctrine be once admitted, and a greater blow will be dealt to personal security than any given to it for a century." [14] When, in *Ex parte McCardle*,[15] the majority of the Court voted to postpone consideration of the military imprisonment of a newspaper editor under the Reconstruction Acts, Field joined Justice Grier in a vigorous protest. "It is a case," said Grier, "that involves the liberty and rights not only of the appellant, but of millions of our fellow citizens." [16] Said Field: "I am of the same opinion with my brother Grier." Field, then, seems to have been uniformly on the side of individual freedom in these war and early reconstruction cases.

Meanwhile, the question of Chinese immigration was creating a furor on the west coast. The men who were carving out a railway empire in that area had employed Chinese laborers in great numbers, partly because they could be persuaded to accept wages far lower than whites could live on. The rankling bitterness against "the mongol horde" broke out during the fifties and sixties in a rash of anti-Chinese legislation, and the validity of such laws was fervently asserted on the one hand and sharply questioned on the other. The case

In re Ah Fong [17] brought the problem to Field's judicial notice. California had passed a law which was designed to prevent the immigration of Chinese prostitutes, but which included within its broad proscriptions a variety of other groups. In a circuit court opinion, Field held the statute unconstitutional as interfering with Congressional control over immigration and as unreasonably discriminating against the "frail child of China landed on our shores." [18]

In 1879, the San Francisco "Queue Ordinance" came before Field in the course of his circuit duties. This seems to have been a wholly malicious measure aimed at Chinese who ran afoul of the law. It consisted simply of the requirement that all male prisoners in the San Francisco jail have their hair cropped to the length of one inch. The Chinese, of course, wore "pigtails." Field invalidated the ordinance under the Fourteenth Amendment, characterizing it as "wanton cruelty." He took judicial notice of the fact that, while the law on its face applied to all prisoners, in practice it was enforced only against the Chinese. Such spiteful little laws as these, he said, were not the proper way to handle the Chinese immigration problem and were "unworthy of a brave and manly people." [19]

One more Chinese decision merits consideration before turning to other matters. Again an ordinance of San Francisco was involved, this time one directed against Orientals engaged in the laundry business in that city. The solid citizens objected to the dirt and smell of the establishments in which this trade was carried on, and they sought to remedy the situation by providing that no license to operate a laundry could be issued unless twelve taxpayers and citizens in the same block supported its issuance. Field voided the ordinance on the ground that it was directed against the laundry business as a whole rather than restricted in application to those laundries which were objectionable.[20] Again he had ranged himself on the side of a minority group under the fire of a hostile majority.

These decisions tell us a good deal about the character of Field's principles during the period they cover. It is true that his motivations in the cases arising out of the war were not altogether unclouded. His brother, David Dudley Field, appeared as counsel in both the *Milligan* and *Cummings* cases, arguing on behalf of the sides for which Stephen Field ultimately voted. The issues in all of the war and reconstruction cases were intertwined with the controversy between radicals and moderates which had split the friends of the triumphant Union cause into bitterly opposed camps. As an exponent of states' rights and as a "loyal Democrat," Field's inclination was to oppose any questionable extension of national power that tended to perpetuate wartime animosities. However, in the Chinese cases there were no such complicating circumstances, and a clear strain of sympathy for the unfortunate and oppressed was revealed. Taking the decisions so far considered, one might infer that Field's attitude toward questions of individual liberty and right was simply an extension of the "sane and balanced" viewpoint reflected in the *Newman* case. There was the same tendency to be guided by the essence of the situation rather than its externals, the same basically humane approach to the problem of social control. His humanitarianism was not, indeed, of the type common to social reformers, who often identify themselves with the sufferer. It smacked rather of *noblesse oblige*, a sort of paternalistic attitude toward those who are put upon, a proprietary air toward constitutional rights. But this is not to disparage the sentiment. It only goes to demonstrate that a consciousness of differences in capacity among men need not lead to a dog-eat-dog political philosophy.

Meanwhile, however, in another line of opinions, Field was spelling out his concept of rights as related to private property and economic freedom. The story begins with his dissent in the *Legal Tender Cases*.[21] In *Hepburn v. Griswold*,[22] Chief Justice Chase, speaking for a four-man majority, had invalidated the Legal Tender Acts insofar as they made greenbacks acceptable for payment of debts incurred before their passage. The controversy over the question was fraught with sectional bitterness, but the crucial problem it raised was one of economic justice, since the decision favored the creditor's interests. In the following year (1871), two new justices having been appointed, the Court undertook to reconsider the question and reversed the *Hepburn* decision. Field dissented at great length. To put it briefly, he argued that it had not been necessary to make the greenbacks mandatory legal tender in order to ensure their circulation; hence, in requiring their acceptance as payment for debts, the Congress had exceeded its delegated powers. But the real reason the acts were invalid, of course, was not that they technically overpassed the government's constitutional authority, but that they were unjust. On the doctrine advanced by the majority, Congress might borrow gold on the faith of the United States and repay the debt in paper money. "I am not willing to admit that the Constitution, the boast and glory of our country, would sanction or permit any such legislation. Repudiation in any form, or to any extent, would be dishonor, and for the commission of this public crime no warrant, in my judgment, can ever be found in that instrument." [23] He was undisturbed by the somewhat embarrassing fact that the contract clause of Article I, Section 10, does not apply as a restriction on the national government. "For acts of flagrant injustice . . . there is no authority in any legislative body, even though not restrained by any express constitutional prohibition. For as there are unchangeable principles of right and morality, without which society would be impossible, and men would be but wild beasts preying upon each other, so there are fundamental principles of eternal justice, upon the existence of which all constitutional government is founded, and without which government would be an intolerable and hateful tyranny." [24]

Thus in the familiar language of American democracy, Justice Field set forth his defense of property rights. But in both the Test Oath and Legal Tender decisions he had been plagued by the difficulty that no specific constitutional clause really supported his position. When the *Slaughter-House Cases* [25] came before the Court, however, it appeared that this difficulty had been removed by his archenemies, the radicals. He tried therefore to assimilate his concept of property rights and economic liberty to the privileges or immunities clause of the Fourteenth Amendment. The majority of the Court upheld the Louisiana state law granting a slaughtering monopoly. Justice Field dissented at length.

The privileges and immunities of citizens of the United States he said, are defined in part by the action of Congress in passing the Civil Rights Act, for one of the purposes of the Fourteenth Amendment was to obviate objections to that law. It is important to remember that he makes this point, so as to contrast his argument in this case with his position in the *Civil Rights Cases* a few years later. But the term is really defined, he went on to say, not by Congress or by any court, but by morality itself. The monopoly grant which the majority upheld violates "one of the most sacred and imprescriptible rights of man." For the Fourteenth Amendment was intended to give practical effect to the "declaration of 1776 of inalienable rights, rights which are the gift of the Creator, which the law does not confer, but only recognizes." As to what rights may be included within the terms of the amendment, he is not altogether clear. But it is certain that "all monopolies in any known trade or manufacture are an invasion of these privileges, for they encroach upon the liberty of citizens to acquire property and pursue happiness." [26] For that matter, the monopoly would be invalid even if the Fourteenth Amendment had never been ratified. For "grants of exclusive privileges, such as is made by the act in question, are opposed to the whole theory of free government, and it requires no aid from any bill of rights to render them void."

It is noteworthy that Field, although a Democrat and a defender of states' rights, was here arguing for an interpretation of the Fourteenth Amendment which would drastically curtail the sovereignty of the states. Evidently, the desirability of protecting economic rights outweighed in his mind the disadvantage of detracting from state autonomy. It is also important to observe that he was attempting to bring a substantive protection for economic liberty into the Constitution by way of the privileges or immunities clause. This effort was doomed to failure. By the time of the *Munn* decision,[27] however, the logic of events and the arguments of counsel had helped him to see the possibilities of the due process clause, and he was ready to claim for that clause the same far-reaching effect he had attributed to the other.

Reference was made earlier to the significance of this dissent in the development of American constitutional law. It is chiefly interesting here for the light it casts on Field's now fully ripened concept of economic liberty. His opinions on the legal-tender question had, after all, merely asserted the right of a man to be repaid in the coin he had loaned, while in the *Slaughter-House* opinion he had defended the common-law privilege of an individual to follow his trade without arbitrary prohibitions. It was a step forward to maintain, as Field did in the *Munn* case, that the Fourteenth Amendment relieves property from any public obligations save those recognized by the law of nuisances. "I deny," he said categorically, "the power of any legislature under our government to fix the price one shall receive for his property of any kind." The term "property" in the due process clause should be given the most liberal possible construction. It refers not only to the physical possession of and title to property, but to the use and income of property as well. The police power cannot justify rate-fixing, because the question of price is unrelated to the objectives of the police power. The owner of property should be free to do as he wills subject only to "the general and rational principle that every person ought so to use his property as not to injure his neighbors." [28]

What we have here is of course an extreme form of the myopia that seems to have afflicted so many converts to this conservative ideology: an inability to recognize the practical truths behind the legal and theoretical fictions of "laissez faire." In later years the same kind of factitious logic supported the argument that statutes outlawing "yellow-dog contracts," child labor, and starvation wages invade the contractual freedom of both employer and worker, although "freedom" applied to the circumstances of these workers is an empty term. It is tempting to regard such arguments as insincere, based on a cynical disregard of social facts, but the explanation must go deeper. The roots of the notion are found in a seldom-stated but nevertheless dominant conviction that the property right is the real basis of social morality, a point of view which inevitably clouds the perception of all associated political questions. The principle *sic utere tuo ut alienum non laedas* which Field invoked was on any rational basis an argument for and not against the regulation of rates of the Chicago grain elevators. Field could see it otherwise only because he had implicitly accepted the proposition that economic freedom transcends all other considerations. Property can be regulated in the interests of the public welfare, but — by hypothesis — the regulation of price cannot serve that interest. For price and profit are the core of the free enterprise system, and to restrict them is to attack the system itself. However much accoutered in Jeffersonian language, this is, in essence, the dogma of Sumnerism.

Just such an atrophy of social insight follows naturally from the broad property-right concept embodied in Field's *Munn* dissent. For in his calculus the property right is now defined so liberally that it tends to become exclusive, by a sort of Gresham's law of ideological currency. To anyone holding such an exalted notion of the scope and importance of economic freedom, it becomes more and more difficult to acknowledge the human claims that may be advanced against it or, finally, to recognize that human rights have any real standing in the scale of social values. The materialization of standards which characterizes the age has translated justice into "free enterprise" terms. And insofar as the democratic tradition is carried forward in the Fieldian value system, that tradition loses its humane quality and becomes identified with "laissez faire" conservatism. Field's balanced view of social interests, his concern for the rights of the human as distinguished from the corporate individual, could not be maintained in company with his developed concept of economic liberty. Human rights must give way when they conflict with the rights of the property owner. And, even when there is no such conflict, individual rights are taken less and less seriously. From the moment it is conceded that economic liberty is the *main* value to be considered in social questions, the way is prepared for the conclusion that it is the *only* value really worth bothering about.

Thus it is possible to trace in Field's opinions a gradual lessening of concern for human rights in general as he follows out the implications of the conservative ethic. There is no reason to doubt his sincerity in the civil liberties decisions of the early postwar period or in the Chinese cases. But the weathervanes of conservative doctrine were pointed in another direction, and as the age wore on the old value lost their

force. Neither by training nor disposition was Field one to
adopt a faith halfheartedly. Having seen the Truth he embraced it; and, under the corroding influence of the Gilded
Age, Field the individualist became Field the economic individualist: the humane elements of his credo were sloughed
away.

The first of his later civil liberties decisions that needs
concern us is *Ex parte Virginia*,[29] a case arising under the
"equal protection clause" of the Fourteenth Amendment. A
Virginia county judge had been indicted on the federal charge
that he had discriminated for reasons of race or color in
choosing qualified jurors. Such discrimination was forbidden
by the Civil Rights Act, and the majority of the Court held
that Congress possessed the constitutional authority to pass
that law in pursuance of the Fourteenth Amendment. Justice
Field, however, argued that the law exceeded the bounds of
national power and unduly invaded the sphere of powers
reserved to the states. His opinion includes an elaborate
analysis of the amendment's meaning, from which it becomes
clear that its clauses were designed to enact the Fieldian concept of a good society into the law of the land. As for the equal
protection clause in particular, "it opens the courts of the
country to everyone, on the same terms, for the security of his
person, the prevention and redress of wrongs, and the enforcement of contracts . . . it allows no impediments to the
acquisition of property and the pursuit of happiness, to which
all are not subjected . . . it leaves political rights or such as
arise from the form of government and its administration, as
they stood previous to its adoption." [30]

Field had based his dissent in the *Slaughter-House Cases*
in part on the intent of the framers as revealed in Congressional debates prior to the passage of the Fourteenth Amendment. In the *Virginia* case, he avoids such an inquiry. Absent
too in this opinion, where civil rather than property rights are

at issue, is the insistence on a generally broad interpretation of the amendment. In the *Slaughter-House* dissent, he had urged that the whole galaxy of rights should be gathered under the protection of the federal judiciary. Now, however, it seems there is a distinction between civil and "political" rights, and it is maintained that the latter have no relation to the purposes of the amendment. As for the enforcement clause, it is construed so narrowly as to have no meaning at all. "The provision authorizing Congress to enforce [rights] by appropriate legislation does not enlarge their scope, nor confer any authority which would not have existed independently of it." [31] One might ask why the enforcement clause was appended to the amendment if the powers it conferred existed already. And the interpretation contradicts the evidence of the debates — directly cited by Field in the *Slaughter-House* dissent — that the Fourteenth Amendment was designed to ensure the constitutionality of the Civil Rights Acts.

These are perhaps matters of detail. The important point to be noted here is that when civil rights stand alone, dissociated from the issue of property, the amendment is construed as narrowly as possible. Field's language is drawn from the states' rights school, as befits an aspirant to public office under the aegis of the Democratic party. Always politically ambitious, he was beginning at this time to dream of the Presidency, and his long and somewhat pointless discussion of the history and nature of the federal system was obviously calculated for political appeal. But the sovereignty of the states is apparently ultimate only when civil rights are in question; it must bow when economic liberty is involved. Nor is the dichotomy he offers between civil and political rights very meaningful. A Negro condemned by a white jury might well ask what civil rights are, if the right to a fair trial is not included among them.

Whatever else may have been wrong with it, Field's dissent in the *Virginia* case "boosted his reputation tremendously in Virginia," as his biographer tells us.[32] That reputation was further enhanced, though his title as a champion of human rights was somewhat clouded, by other opinions in the same field. In *Strauder v. West Virginia*,[33] the Court invalidated a state law which in terms excluded Negroes from jury service. Field dissented on the grounds stated in *Ex parte Virginia*. The *Strauder* situation was somewhat different, however, in that no federal act was involved, and the plaintiff was simply demanding that the Court set aside a state law directly contravening the equal protection clause. Thus the issue was more closely analogous to that posed in the *Slaughter-House* case. The only difference was that a human life was at stake rather than economic liberty. Apparently, however, the civil-political distinction was enough to resolve the question for Field.

Finally, in *Virginia v. Rives*,[34] during the same Court term, Field had his way on the Negro juror issue as he was to have his way on so many issues in this constitutional period. The Court decided that a Negro defendant had no positive right to demand that Negroes serve on the jury trying him, so long as no overt discrimination could be shown. This ruling deprived the *Strauder* decision of most of its effect. Field concurred, to be sure, but he felt called upon to write a separate opinion, enlarging on some of the points he had made previously. The mere fact that no members of his own class are found on the jury does not mean, said Field, that the accused is being denied equal protection of the laws. "Women are not allowed to sit on juries; are they thereby denied the equal protection of the laws? Persons over sixty years of age are disqualified as jurors, yet no one will pretend that they do not enjoy the equal protection of the laws."[35] Neither will anyone pretend, of course, as Field might have pointed out, that a regional prejudice exists against women or the aged. But the existence of such a prejudice is outside the range of judicial cognizance. The conception of what factors a judge may properly consider had altered in more than one respect since the *Newman* decision in California days.

After these opinions, it is something less than surprising that Field concurred in the Court's attenuation of the enforcement clause in the *Civil Rights Cases*.[36] Here it was decided, with only Justice Harlan dissenting, that the Fourteenth Amendment's prohibitions applied only against states. Individual rights could not therefore be protected by Congress against impairment by private persons. Again, as in the jury cases, Justice Field's regard for the rights of the individual was subordinated to other considerations. And again Field's point of view prevailed on the Court, for the narrow construction of the enforcement clause set forth here closely resembles the interpretation he advanced in the *Ex parte Virginia* dissent. And by the Court's opinion the enforcement clause was rendered almost meaningless.

Field's concept of the relation between civil rights and the Fourteenth Amendment becomes even more tenuous in *Hurtado v. California*[37] a few years later. When the Court, in *Walker v. Sauvinet*,[38] had held that a jury trial in suits at common law was not required by the Fourteenth Amendment, Justices Field and Clifford had dissented without opinion. The property rights of the appellant were of course involved. In the *Hurtado* decision, however, a murder indictment had been returned by information rather than by grand jury, and the defendant had been sentenced to hang. The Court decided that nothing in the Fourteenth Amendment prevented California from so modifying criminal procedures, and Mr. Justice Matthews went on to argue that the liberties protected by the first eight amendments to the national Constitution are not embodied in the Fourteenth. Field concurred

in this opinion in spite of its radical departure from the view
he had taken in the *Slaughter-House* and *Munn* cases. It is
also interesting to compare Field's solicitude in the Test Oath
cases for the "universally recognized" principles of the common law heretofore "supposed to be fundamental and unchangeable" with the tolerance for innovation expressed in
the *Hurtado* decision. As time goes on, it becomes more and
more difficult to say just what those "civil rights" are which
the biographer tells us are deserving of protection "as a matter of special moment."

Finally, in the later cases involving the Chinese problem,
evidence can be found to support the view that a lighter
weight is being assigned to individual rights in the Fieldian
scales of social value. His previous decisions had outraged
his fellow Californians, who saw them as gratuitous interference with state autonomy, and a vicious campaign of vilifica-
tion was launched against Field. For a time he stood firm. It
may be inferred that he failed to sense the extent of the public wrath, or it may be inferred more charitably that he was
reluctant to bow before it on a matter of principle. Whatever
the reason for his hesitation may have been, it is certain that
he delayed his turnabout too long to salvage his political
fortunes. In 1884, the Democratic state convention in California repudiated Field's presidential candidacy by the re-
sounding vote of 453 to 19, and his Chinese decisions played
no small part in the arguments against him. Thereafter his
opinions in cases involving the Chinese began to follow a
sharply different course.

Only one of these later cases need be cited to make the
point, especially since Professor Swisher has traced this re-
versal in some detail.[39] *Barbier v. Connolly* [40] involved a
San Francisco ordinance which prohibited workers in public
laundries in certain sections of the city from pursuing their
occupation between ten in the evening and six in the morn-

ing. Field wrote the decision of the Court, holding that no discrimination against the Chinese had been shown. Nothing on the face of the ordinance, he said, suggested that it was aimed at the Chinese: "The provision is purely a police regulation. . . And it would be an extraordinary usurpation of the authority of a municipality, if a federal tribunal should undertake to supervise such regulations." [41] This may be true enough; the decision, in fact, would be unnoteworthy were it not for Field's previous record on similar issues. In the "Queue Ordinance" case cited above, he had been willing to invade municipal authority when an ordinance operated against a particular class, whether or not the intention to discriminate appeared on the face of the law; and in the *Quong Woo* case he had attacked the "miserable pretense" that the laundry business is somehow dangerous to morals or public safety.[42] Now however, and in the majority of the Chinese opinions that follow, questions of doubt are resolved in favor of public authority and against the individual rights of Chinese.

The tracing of this apparently inconsistent course in Field's opinions concerning civil liberty is not of course worth while if it proves only that his long years of judicial service were not marked by a perfect harmony of viewpoint. Few jurists maintain faultless consistency, and it is surely doubtful whether the law would be well served if they attempted to do so. But the disparities in Field's decisions are instructive because they reflect a shift in value premises which is characteristic not only of Field but of his age. He began his judicial career, if the evidence may be believed, with a general bias in favor of individual rights, and for a time no difficulties appeared. Before very long, however, this value system was complicated by discordances — his own growing political ambition and a special emphasis on the sanctity of economic freedom. Without much difficulty, we can deduce from the preceding discussion just how these diverse elements were ranked in the value hierarchy that finally emerged. Evidently, the property right is the transcendent value; political ambition ranks next when it is relevant; and the cause of human or civil rights is subordinate to these higher considerations.

II

We are now in a position to assay Justice Field from the point of view of his impact on constitutional history and his place in the American conservative tradition. It is perhaps best to begin by bringing together in summary form some of the points that have been made in this discussion of his judicial positions and his personal character. From what has been said of his early training, some guesses can be made about the influences that helped to form the man. The long hours on the church benches and around the fireside at home undoubtedly left their imprint; the Williams of Mark Hopkins may have reinforced a dogmatic attitude toward ethical questions; the study of law, as that discipline was understood in America of the 1840's, must have helped to perpetuate the same illusion. Then, as he approached intellectual maturity, Field was thrust into the frontier world of the California gold rush, different in so many respects from the environment he was bred to, yet curiously similar in the habits of mind it engendered and the precepts it taught. Meanwhile, and with progressive forcefulness, the feeling must have been growing that he and his brothers had the stuff of greatness.

It is impossible, of course, to know how decisive these conditioning elements were in forging the mature personality of Stephen Field. We can only point to them and the man who evolved and suggest a possible relationship. Insofar as the suggestion is valid, then, it can be said that these influences produced a man who was accustomed to assess problems of right and wrong in absolute terms, who acknowledged no area of moral uncertainty. They begat a consciousness of personal superiority which sometimes degenerated into mere vanity, but at other times seems to have fortified a concept of personal stewardship, of seignorial obligation. And this frame of reference in turn led Field to adopt an air of righteousness in setting forth his opinions, a pose which was perhaps infuriating to those who disagreed, but which gave his pronouncements great force and conviction. It made him quick to adopt the extreme position while his fellows yet hesitated; it gave him courage, garbed in Truth as he was, to cling stubbornly to that position even when it seemed legally untenable.

This is the complex of personal characteristics that Field carried with him into the Civil War period and out of it through the Gilded Age. Again, we cannot know what factors, other than the time-spirit itself, may have helped to mold him further. But it does appear that the fifteen years from 1860 to 1875 gave a new turn to Field's beliefs concerning social morality: they provided him with an ideal to replace his eroded religious faith; they supplied new saints for him to venerate. And we know that the age was one in which capitalism emerged triumphant, in which American values were transformed, in which economic liberty was exalted.

The personality traits that have been noted and the ideal that Field embraced combine to explain the special place he merits in the history of American conservatism. For in Field's opinions we find the gospel of wealth framed in absolute moral terms. The gospel is not different in its essentials from the frankly materialistic rationale of William Graham Sumner. There is the same disregard for humane values, the same worship of success, the same standard of individual merit. The Fieldian conceptions lead to the same dark conclusions regarding popular government, the same implication that society should be organized by and for a natural elite. But instead of resting on a base in dubious scientism, the values of Field claim the status of religious verities; they are self-evident, not empirical; they are "moral" in the old, understandable sense of the word.

Again, because Field is Field, the continuity of the entrepreneurial philosophy with the American democratic tradition is not only asserted but insisted upon. If the new truths are confirmed by revelation rather than by factual proof, there is no need to abandon the timeworn American mythology of natural rights. The Declaration of Independence, the evangel of that tradition, is called to the defense of the conservative cause; and the dogma of "laissez faire" becomes synonymous with Jeffersonian democracy.

Finally, all that has been said here about the personality of Field, about his social philosophy, and about the ethic that underlies it, helps to explain the extraordinary influence he seems to have exerted on American constitutional development. The Court came to occupy, by the end of the nineteenth century, a social position so nearly identical to that urged by Field that even he could hardly have asked a more flattering epitaph. The explanation is, of course, that Field had cast his appeals to the Court in terms which the other justices ultimately found irresistible. The conservative value system that he espoused was their own at bottom. Field troubled their consciences by urging them to do what they already more than half believed they ought to do. Moreover, he confronted them with an unescapable moral issue, giving them to understand that both God and the Founding Fathers execrated judges who shirked their duty. Something of Field's self-assurance must have communicated itself to men who were thinking in the same frame of reference without quite knowing it; and his insistence was such that he gave them no peace. Field could not have influenced a Court to whom his views were antithetical, but to the Court of the Gilded Age he spoke as a prophet. His personality, his mental habits, and his ideals were remarkably adapted to the task of leading opinion in an age that had lost its way.

six

CONSERVATISM AND THE AMERICAN MIND:

ANDREW CARNEGIE

I

There are many ways in which one might characterize the nineteenth-century movement of thought that I have called modern conservatism. From one viewpoint, it might be seen as a reassertion of the American idea of progress, a reinterpretation in machine-age terms of traditional beliefs in the destiny of America. From another perspective, it could be recognized as a largely successful effort to redefine such cabalistic symbols as "rights," "liberty," and "equality," and to invoke them in defense of business enterprise. In still a third sense, this conservatism might be understood as a campaign to assign the role of social leadership to the successful business entrepreneur, to focus the American proclivity for hero-worship upon the "self-made" economic man.

No matter which of these variations is being considered, however, it should be recognized that all depend upon the same basic conservative theme, which defines good and right in materialist rather than humane terms. Without the support of that central assumption, the conservative case largely fails; but insofar as the assumption gains general acceptance, the whole argument is strengthened. The measure of conservatism's success in nineteenth-century America was the extent of popular devotion to its underlying materialist ideal. I have already referred to the ambivalence in American political motivations which arose from the conflict between antithetical standards of value, of the confusion in democratic thinking which was fostered by the conservative restatement of the Jeffersonian tradition. By and large, I have suggested, the period was marked by the ascendency of conservative dogmas, the triumph of a materialist ethic over American democratic ideals.

But it should go without saying that this conservative victory was never unconditional: old ideals continued to smoulder and, after about 1900, began to exert increased pressure on those who formulated public policy. Nor was even this qualified control over popular opinion established without a struggle. The spirit of humanitarian democracy resisted the apostasy that was forced upon it, and although this resistance was often incoherent and irresolute, it had to be reckoned with. Any real understanding of the nature of political thought in postwar America depends on an analysis of both the fact of conservative dominance and the process by which it was achieved.

We have already observed this process at work in the mental development of William Graham Sumner and Stephen J. Field, an academician and a jurist, respectively. It is true, however, that Sumner's native bias in favor of both materialism and capitalism was so great that no really fundamental transposition of values was necessary; he is interesting not so much for his acceptance of the new postulates as for the way he worked out their implications. Field, too, was somewhat atypical. Although his full conversion seems to have come late in life, it was so wholehearted when it did occur that few doubts remained to plague him. There is no reason to believe that either of these men was torn by a moral conflict.

If for both Sumner and Field the struggle between ma-

terialism and idealism was easy to resolve, for the majority
of their fellow-countrymen the problem was more complex.
The attachment to traditional values was too deep-seated to
be lightly set aside, and while the whole weight and prestige
of industrial capitalism was ranged in support of the materialist standard, on the other side was the tradition summed
up in the maxim that man does not live by bread alone. The
thoroughgoing conservative, like Field, simply rationalized
the moral dilemma away by identifying the material and the
moral norms. The more moderate — and therefore more typical — American tended in the same direction, but he found
the paradox more troublesome; and the story of political
opinion in the Gilded Age is in part a tale of inner dissent,
of an attempt to reconcile contradictory standards of value.

It is this ambivalence in American thought during the
period that has led certain observers to qualify their judgment regarding its basic materialism. Santayana thus diag-
noses a malady which threatens the American character:

The pioneer must devote himself to preparations; he must
work for the future, and it is healthy and dutiful of him to love
his work for its own sake. At the same time, unless reference to an
ultimate purpose is at least virtual in all his activities, he runs the
danger of becoming a living automaton, vain and ignominious in
its mechanical constancy. Idealism about work can hide an intense
materialism about life. Man, if he is a rational being, cannot live
by bread alone nor be a labourer merely; he must eat and work in
view of an ideal harmony which overarches all his days, and which
is realized in the way they hang together, or in some ideal issue
which they have in common. Otherwise, though his technical
philosophy may call itself idealism, he is a materialist in morals;
he esteems things, and esteems himself for mechanical uses and
energies.[1]

Yet here and there, Santayana goes on, he has heard "a groan
at the perpetual incubus of business and shrill society. . .

When the senses are sharp, as they are in the American, they are already half liberated, already a joy in themselves; and when the heart is warm, like this, and eager to be just, its ideal destiny can hardly be doubtful. It will not be always merely pumping and working; time and its own pulses will lend it wings." [2] James Bryce, a less subtle intellect perhaps, but a conscientious observer of America, is infected with something of its own "sanguine spirit"; and while acknowledging the national devotion to Number and the preoccupation with commercial standards of value, he retains high hopes that the Republic is yet on the road to achievement of its original ideals.[3] Finally, Walt Whitman:

I say we had best look our times and lands searchingly in the face, like a physician diagnosing some deep disease. Never was there, perhaps, more hollowness at heart than at present, and here in the United States. Genuine belief seems to have left us. The underlying principles of the States are not honestly believed in . . . it is as if we were somehow being endowed with a vast and more and more thoroughly-appointed body, and then left with little or no soul.[4]

Still, in the same essay: "I hail with joy the oceanic, variegated, intense practical energy, the demand for facts, even the business materialism of the current age, our States." For these are to be, in the American future Whitman envisions, the fuel that feeds the flame of the soul. Americans are not only the "most materialistic and money-making people ever known," but the "most emotional, spiritualistic and poetry-loving people also."

Whatever may have been their intimations for the future, however, it was evident even to these observers that materialism was, for the time being, in the saddle and riding the age. That there remained remnants of the old value system, that even in his preoccupation with "mechanical constancy" the American was never wholly insensible to other

ideals — these were good signs. But they underlined by contrast the really powerful sway which the business ethic
had established, they made the temporary triumph of material values all the more clear. For the majority of Americans,
no objective seemed so imperative as material prosperity, few
standards of merit were more reliable than the standard of
pecuniary success.

A particularly fruitful area for observing this dualism
of American ideals is in the pattern of contemporary attitudes
toward that master symbol of proficiency, the successful
businessman. The whole aim of extreme conservative thinking was to exalt this personage as the paragon of modern
virtues. One of the principal inferences from Social Darwinism, as we have seen in tracing the ideas of Sumner, is
that a man's social worth is directly proportionate to the
amount of capital he has accumulated, that the tools of the
community, as Carlyle put it, belong in the hands of those
who can handle them. Sumner bases his argument for un-
limited accumulation of wealth on utility; Field grounds it in
the moral law. But the arguments, whatever form they take,
are secondary; they are rationalizations of the proposition
that "nothing succeeds like success."

To America at large, the successful businessman never
quite assumed the heroic proportions the radical conservatives would assign to him. The nation seemed quick to criticize the money barons when some of their more knavish
antics were exposed to the public eye. Several of them —
Gould, Fisk, Rockefeller, and even Carnegie — were at one
time or another subjected to popular obloquy and, instead
of being canonized as saints, were stigmatized as wrongdoers.
As Wecter has shown, real adulation was reserved for other
types: for the military leader Grant, until he tarnished his
reputation with shady business connections; for the democratic hero Lincoln, whose human appeal was irresistible.[5]

Bryce scouted foreign premonitions that America was evolving an aristocracy of wealth. "The feeling of the American public towards the very rich is, so far as a stranger can judge, one of curiosity and wonder rather than of respect." [6]

But if America was sometimes ready to blame the men of big business for their more flagrant depredations, we must remember that it was quick to forgive them as well. Rockefeller, once "the most hated man in America," died full of years, honored by the nation. Carnegie was eulogized as "Saint Andrew" not many years after Homestead; and Pope Pius X echoed the sentiments of America when he described Morgan as "a great and good man." The fact is that the millionaire businessman occupied a good deal more exalted place in the American imagination than Bryce would accord to him. It is true that the average American did not, even in the Gilded Age, worship money *per se*. He worshiped rather material accomplishment, production, quantity. That is why, as Wecter remarks, Henry Ford the producer, rather than the speculator, has been the most fervently admired among American business titans. But in a civilization that recognizes only material achievement, "getting things done" and "making money" are not often distinguishable. And if the pull of nobler deals was too strong to allow any businessman a place beside Lincoln and Lee, it was not strong enough to prevent the entrepreneur from assuming as of right the practical leadership of the community. A nagging intimation persisted that the material standard of goodness might not be altogether final, but it was only a faint discord in the main theme.

And for great numbers of Americans this discord was harmonized by the feeling that material advance would open the way to realization of the more intangible aims of traditional democracy. On a relatively sophisticated level, this idea was nurtured by Social Darwinism and orthodox economics; on a lower plane, it was less articulate and rational, but no less comforting. The notion allowed men to avoid thinking about democratic ends by postponing them; it permitted them to conform to a materialist behavior code without acknowledging it as final. Thus inner doubts, where they existed, could be resolved. If any question yet remained regarding the compatibility of the new capitalism with the traditional democratic ethic, this doctrine might be said to settle it. By keeping their eyes on the main chance, by accumulating wealth as rapidly as possible, Americans might serve not only the latter-day deities of the market place but the old gods as well. And with this rationalization of the fundamental material bias, the last real barrier to the absorption of democracy in conservatism was removed.

It will be observed, however, that this solution presupposes a highly optimistic outlook upon the future of both capitalism and democracy. It postulates a constantly improving standard of well-being throughout the community, an improvement which will in turn create conditions progressively more favorable to the flowering of the individual personality. And no such consoling assurance could be found in the writings of William Graham Sumner. His willingness to face up to the implications of empirical fact had led him to a skeptical conclusion; he had little faith in the religion of human betterment. Life is hard and will remain so; democratic idealism is merely a product of the favorable man–land ratio. When that ratio shifts in accordance with the Malthusian law, democracy will pass away and be revealed as a temporary aberration. And Field too, in his later years, was full of dark forebodings. Thus the new conservatism needed, as I have said earlier, not only an underlying rationale and scientific base, which Sumner gave it, not only a moral and democratic gloss, which Field supplied, but also an optimistic overtone which would make it congenial to the American temperament. America could not accept a philosophy of abnegation and gloom. The national dream was of a bright and expanding future.

II

In his life and in his opinions, Andrew Carnegie (1835–1919) exemplifies these general characteristics of postwar American thought. If the age was troubled by a conflict of ideals, so too was Carnegie troubled. If his contemporaries sometimes questioned the religion of dollar-chasing, so did Carnegie question and even, in his soul-searching moments, condemn it. And if the age sometimes doubted that the successful businessman was his own justification for being, Andrew Carnegie shared these misgivings. But he is consistent with the spirit of his day, not only in his doubts, but in his affirmations. For — again like the Gilded Age — he resolved his ideal conflict in favor of materialism; he devoted himself to the ruthless pursuit of wealth; and he salved the conscience that pricked him by the assurance that, in the long run, everything was for the best. He concealed his abandonment of democratic values even from himself by the pretext that his lust for gain was infused with a deeper social purpose, that the cause of democracy would profit most if Andrew Carnegie and others like him grew as rich as possible, basing this faith on a dauntless optimism compounded partly of Social Darwinism and partly of personal bias. And he lived to enjoy the high regard the nation accorded to the man of wealth whose sins, committed in acquiring his substance, have been absolved by time and good works. To America in general, as for Carnegie himself, the millions of dollars he gave away were payment in full for the account of the previous fifty years.

It is speciously easy to regard Andrew Carnegie either as the model capitalist, employing for the welfare of man the power which wealth had given him, acknowledging and accepting the moral obligations imposed by his position of industrial leadership, or, on the other hand, as a pious hypocrite who talked the language of Christian brotherhood while playing the contemporary game of dog eat dog. If I take neither of these views, it is not because I am concerned with achieving a balanced and moderate interpretation for its own sake, but because Carnegie was actually far more complex than either of these descriptions suggests and because some understanding of his motivations is important to an understanding of the motives of his age. For Carnegie was not, whatever else might be said about him, a "typical" capitalist. He was far more absorbed than most of his peers in the moral problems posed by a burgeoning industrial civilization, or at any rate he was more articulate about them. Nor was he simply buying posterity when he gave away his millions or courting public regard when he wrote his benign essays on behalf of the rights of workingmen and the glories of democracy. The real Carnegie is neither the "Saint Andrew" of Hendrick's biography nor the poseur and self-seeker of Winkler.[7] If he is typical of anything, he is typical of America en masse rather than its financial overlords, and he makes explicit the conflicts and resolutions that characterized the mind of the nation. Thus his conservatism differs from the extremist Fieldian or Sumnerian brand; it is a modification of those uncompromising dogmas and more accurately reflects the true conservative temper of the age.

Carnegie was born in Dunfermline, Scotland, in 1835. Dunfermline was a center of the Scottish weaving industry, and its inhabitants had inherited a strong tradition of political radicalism. In Carnegie's own family this tradition was especially deep-rooted. His paternal grandfather was locally notorious for his radicalism and his contentious spirit. On his mother's side, his grandfather, Thomas Morrison, was almost famous, the recognized leader of reformist movements in Dunfermline, an occasional contributor to William Cobbett's *Political Register*, and even for a time himself editor of a local journal so revolutionary in tone that the Dunfermline printer refused to handle it. This grandfather also organized a "Political Union" among the weavers of the city for "the diffusion of political knowledge, the improvement of national institutions, and, specially, to effect a reform of the Commons House of Parliament." [8] Andrew Carnegie's father, though a milder man, carried on the tradition, speaking before Chartist rallies, which seem to have been almost daily affairs in Dunfermline in the 1840's. Andrew's uncle, the son and namesake of Grandfather Morrison, assumed the leadership in local political discussions when his father died. Gathering with great crowds of unenfranchised workers, he earned the reputation of being one of the most effective political hecklers in Scotland. Though opposed on principle to rick-burning and similar expressions of Chartist discontent, he led in organizing a general strike (called the "Peaceful Cessation from Labor") and was jailed for his pains. "I remember as if it were yesterday," said Carnegie in his autobiography, "being awakened during the night by a tap at the back window by men who had come to inform my parents that my uncle, Bailie Morrison, had been thrown in jail because he had dared to hold a meeting which had been forbidden." [9] "It is not to be wondered at that, nursed amid such surroundings, I developed into a violent young Republican whose motto was 'death to privilege.'" [10]

Some years later, Carnegie was to say of America in *Triumphant Democracy*: "The unity of the American people is further powerfully promoted by the foundation upon which the political structure rests, the equality of the citizen. There is not one shred of privilege to be met with anywhere in all the laws." [11] One wonders what his Chartist forebears would have thought of this judgment. As an American capitalist, Carnegie always professed to cherish his radical heritage. Discovering a handbill which had been printed at the time of the Chartist agitations and which appealed for three hundred pounds to defend his uncle against the charge of conspiracy, he had it framed and "when his Majesty, King Edward, visited Skibo, I showed him the bill, duly framed and hanging on the wall, as my title to nobility." [12] But it is hard to think that the uncle would have been satisfied with the kind of perfect equality that existed in the America of the 1880's, and the nephew must in his heart have had some inkling of this. It seems likely that his contact with the impassioned radicalism of Dunfermline planted impulses in his breast that could never be altogether stifled. Not even the rosy hue which he cast over America in such books as the one quoted could blind him to the fact that something pretty serious was still amiss; he kept searching for panaceas, for a formula that would reconcile his two ideal worlds.

Throughout his life when he speaks of privilege what he means is the privilege of monarchy or aristocracy, based on the accident of birth. This was an excellent straw man to pommel, and his zeal for belaboring the baronage allowed him to ignore the network of genuine privilege on which protected industries like Carnegie Steel subsisted. It was harmless if somewhat silly to assume an attitude of unflinching hostility to feudalism in the American twentieth century, and it is slightly pathetic that even this seems to have been more than half a pose. His writings had made his scorn for the titled great familiar to everyone. "Oh! yes, yes," said the Kaiser when he and Carnegie met. "I have read your books. You do not like kings." [13] But Mark Twain knew better: "He thinks he is a scorner of kings and emperors and dukes, whereas he is like the rest of the human race: a slight attention from one of these can make him drunk for a week and keep his happy tongue wagging for seven years." [14] Nevertheless, his professed antagonism to this brand of privilege helped to preserve Carnegie's picture of himself as the heir of Chartism, even if, in the last analysis, he could never quite deceive his own conscience.

In religion, as in politics, Carnegie's legacy was unorthodox. His father, though reared as a Calvinist, had left the church, and his mother's clan, the Morrisons, had never held with the Shorter Catechism. Though "always reticent on religious subjects," Margaret Carnegie was, according to her son, fascinated by the Unitarianism of William Ellery Channing, whose works she read while the family was still in Scotland. In that land, even in doctrinally emancipated Dunfermline, no youth could altogether escape the shadow of John Knox, and Carnegie tells us: "I well remember that the stern doctrines of Calvinism lay as a terrible nightmare upon me." [15] But as far as can be seen, the oppression was fleeting, and formal religion of any sort never meant much to him. Or rather, formal religion became another whipping-boy, like monarchy and "privilege." His denunciation of theology sometimes shocked sensitive churchgoers, but it gave him increased assurance that he was, as his biographer says, ahead of his time. In his first address as Lord Rector of St. Andrews in 1902, he set forth his own positive creed. "At this period of my life I was all at sea. No creed, no system, reached me, all was chaos. I had outgrown the old and found no substitute. . . Here came to me Spencer and Darwin, whom I read with absorbing interest, until laying down a volume one day I was able to say, 'That settles the question.' " [16] Henceforward he was satisfied that order existed in the universe, and God became for him Spencer's "Inscrutable Essence." It is tempting to find in Carnegie's life a survival of Calvinist notions of original sin for which his benefactions were an unconscious expiation, but the facts

hardly seem to support the idea. He was by no means incapable of spiritual experience (as Sumner, for example, seems
to have been), but his cast of mind was too genial and
optimistic to become entangled in the dour Presbyterian
formulations.

In Dunfermline days, at the feet of Uncle George Lauder, two of his abiding passions were fostered — poetry and
patriotism. The poet at first was of course Burns, and verse
after verse Andrew committed to memory and carried with
him throughout his life. "It is impossible," says Hendrick, "to
over-estimate the influence of the national poet on this particular worshipper." [17] What this presumably means is that
Carnegie drew the precepts by which he lived from sources
like "The Cotter's Saturday Night," a somewhat dubious
proposition, although he says himself in the *Autobiography*
that "the best rules of conduct are in Burns." [18] The important point, so far as this essay is concerned, is that Carnegie's love for Burns, and later for Shakespeare, offers a
hint that he comprehended other realms of being than the
material world of smoke and steel and money-grubbing. His
consciousness that aesthetic values have an important place
in the life of civilized man was not, as it was for Sumner,
a concession to an alien taste, but a real and personal
conviction.

As for patriotism, he drew it in with the air he breathed,
and the sentimental excess of his youthful love for Scotland
is matched only by his later affection for America. It is not
unusual for a young boy, and particularly a Scot, to exult
in his country's glories, but there was something special
about Carnegie's passion. He had a peculiar need, even as a
man, to idealize his environment, and the adulation he early
lavished on Wallace and Robert the Bruce was later dupli-
cated in his hero-worship of Washington and Lincoln. "How
wonderful is the influence of a hero on children," he said

in his autobiography, somewhat self-consciously, because
he knew that his own life would be cited as an example to
schoolboys whose fathers were raised in the Gilded Age.[19]
And all his life he worshiped heroes whose lives were in
sharp contrast to his own industrial career; he looked back
to the great of another time, or he turned to men like Spencer
and Arnold and Morley in his own day, scholars and poets,
not captains of industry. Carnegie wanted to be a hero
himself, and he knew that in some measure the age had made
him one; but the suspicion of something lacking both in the
times and in himself was never quite absent.

As steam machinery was introduced in the weaving industry, the small home producers of Dunfermline found it
more and more difficult to maintain themselves, and Andrew's father, never a great success at business, suffered
with the rest. Things eventually grew so bad that the family
determined to emigrate. The looms were sold, an extra
twenty pounds was borrowed to finance steerage passage,
and the classic Alger-like saga of immigrant boy to industrial
monarch was begun. The future tycoon was then thirteen;
he had a little education, a good deal of natural cleverness,
and a consuming ambition to make his way.

The family went to Allegheny, Pennsylvania, and, though
Andrew's letters home to his beloved uncle, George Lauder,
were full of optimism, the first years were very hard. Father
and son were both employed in the Blackstock Cotton Mill
from six in the morning until six at night, but William Carnegie would not stand it; he was soon back home, working
his individual hand loom and trying to sell his products from
door to door. Andrew stuck it out — he always stuck it out —
graduated to a slightly more remunerative but even more
unpleasant factory job (his pay was $1.65 a week), and
finally to a position as messenger boy in the rapidly developing telegraph industry. Messenger boys in the inspirational

success chronicles of the period were always bright, enterprising lads, and Andrew was the mold from which the casting was made. He knew, as he said in a letter home, that "anyone can get along in this Country." [20] The rags-to-riches narrative was unfolding fast.

By 1851, when he was only fifteen, Andrew had graduated from messenger boy to telegraph operator. No reader of success stories will be startled to learn that he achieved this eminence by rising early and practicing telegraphy before the regular operators had arrived. Meanwhile, still in the tradition of the Industrious Apprentice, he was reading assiduously to improve his mind — Bancroft, Charles Lamb, Macaulay, and Prescott, and of course his lifelong love, Shakespeare. He was already beginning to heap praises on his adopted land, where the liberty and equality envisioned by the People's Charter seemed to him already established. His admiration for American democracy was already unbounded. "For our government is founded upon justice and our creed is that the will of the People is the *source* and their happiness the *end* of all legitimate Government," he said when he was seventeen, in a letter to his cousin.[21] And always he extolled the great material advances of the young nation, the technological and industrial dynamism that intoxicated him as much as American standards of popular liberty. He had no inkling yet that the one might impinge on the other, that America's twin ideals might someday conflict.

In 1853, Carnegie left the telegraph office to work as assistant and clerk to Thomas A. Scott, one of the great names in railroad history and then superintendent of the Scott had advanced to the vice-presidency of the road and Carnegie had moved up to Scott's old place. The salary was $1500 a year, a respectable sum, but Carnegie had already Pennsylvania Railroad's western division. Six years later, begun to lay the foundations of his future wealth on another basis. His first investment had been made, and his position with the railroad was paying off. With becoming candor, Carnegie tells in his autobiography of an incident that occurred about this time. While riding on a passenger train, he had been buttonholed by T. T. Woodruff, inventor of the sleeping car, who was trying to persuade some railroad to pioneer its development. Carnegie agreed to use his influence, Scott was receptive, and "after this, Mr. Woodruff, greatly to my surprise, asked me if I would not join him in the new enterprise and offered me an eighth interest in the venture." [22]

The early history of Carnegie's fortune is shrouded in some mystery, but it is probable that such deals as this played a conspicuous part. They were not frowned upon in the business world of his time, and since Carnegie tells the tale in a life chronicle that uniformly portrays its author as blameless, we may assume that he saw no harm in it. In 1865, he resigned from the railroad, because, as he tells us, "my investments now began to require so much of my personal attention . . . I was determined to make a fortune and I saw no means of doing this honestly at any salary the railroad company could afford to give, and I would not do it by indirection." [23] It would be interesting to know what he means by "indirection." His interests were now substantial enough to demand all his time, yet his salary had never been more than $1800 a year. This remarkable circumstance "might lead the innocent minded," as Mark Sullivan is quoted as saying, "to look upon Carnegie as the outstanding example of Scotch thrift in all history." [24]

The fact is that Carnegie was conducting his business life in accordance with the going code, and there is no real evidence that he ever conducted it any differently. His interest in the Keystone Bridge Company, which earned him

$15,000 in 1868, was acquired without a cent of outlay "in return for services rendered in its promotion." [25] And he was receiving returns from the company in 1863, two years before its actual incorporation and while he himself was still an official of the railroad which was one of its principal customers.[26] This was the way things were done, it was how young men got ahead, and "nothing," as he says in an unguarded moment of self-revelation in his autobiography, "could be allowed to interfere for a moment with my business career." [27] With only occasional twinges of regret, he was accepting the world of fact and finance together with its standards.

The story of the growth of the Carnegie steel interests after 1865 has been told too often, with varying degrees of objectivity, to be recapitulated in any detail here. A few of the landmarks in that history must be touched upon, however, for the light they throw on the man who was the protagonist of the epic. As he was swept along by the passion for money-getting, he devised practices and techniques which were in startling contrast to the humanitarian sentiments of his preachments. And the point is that Carnegie did preach. On a wide range of subjects, he laid down the law to a respectfully listening populace, and most of his sermons were dotted with pious homilies and declarations of good intention. He was, by his own admission, "the staunch friend of labor, the benefactor of mankind." So he wished to be regarded, and according to this high standard he must be judged. The malefactions of other contemporary captains of finance can be in part excused on the ground that they professed no pietistic sentiments; but Andrew Carnegie cannot be let off so easily.

Few of America's great industrialists have provided posterity with so intimate a glimpse of their souls as is found in a memorandum written in Carnegie's own hand when he was thirty-three. The document might be said to epitomize the dilemma of America itself when it began dimly to apprehend the pitfalls of the new industrial age:

St. Nicholas Hotel, New York
December, 1868

Thirty-three and an income of $50,000 per annum! By this time two years I can arrange all my business as to secure at least $50,000 per annum. Beyond this never earn — make no effort to increase fortune, but spend the surplus each year for benevolent purposes. Cast aside business forever, except for others.

Settle in Oxford and get a thorough education, making the acquaintance of literary men — this will take three years' active work — pay especial attention to speaking in public. Settle then in London and purchase a controlling interest in some newspaper or live review and give the general management of it attention, taking a part in public matters, especially those connected with education and improvement of the poorer classes.

Man must have an idol — the amassing of wealth is one of the worst species of idolatry — no idol more debasing than the worship of money. Whatever I engage in I must push inordinately; therefore should I be careful to choose that life which will be the most elevating in its character. To continue much longer overwhelmed by business cares and with most of my thoughts wholly upon the way to make more money in the shortest time, must degrade me beyond hope of permanent recovery. I will resign business at thirty-five, but during the ensuing two years I wish to spend the afternoons in receiving instruction and in reading systematically.[28]

One of Carnegie's friendly biographers, who cites this memorandum as evidence that he was thinking even then along the lines later set forth in *The Gospel of Wealth*, tells us: "Almost every item of the ideal existence, as it appeared to the young man, he ultimately carried out." [29] But this misses the central point of the avowal, which is that the pursuit of wealth, unless soon cast aside, "must degrade me beyond hope of permanent recovery." In this private moment (the document was never intended for publication), and in how many others we cannot know, Carnegie realized what the materialist preoccupation of the age was doing to him; he was aware that he could not have the best of two worlds. The other world, the one represented by these resolutions, was the one he knew was good; but the business world, with its idolatry of money and tangible success, held a fascination for him which was ultimately irresistible. So he did not cast business aside. On the contrary, his tendency to "push inordinately" carried him along the same road for thirty more years, though this document alone would be enough to show that he was never untroubled.

"Save for the fortuity of circumstances," says one biographer of Carnegie, "he, not John D. Rockefeller, would symbolize ruthlessness in business." [30] There is much, in fact, to support the charge. Carnegie's method of handling supervisory personnel, for example, was so calculatingly inhumane that some found life in his service impossible to bear. He encouraged a spirit of unfriendly competition between his department heads and partners and goaded them remorselessly into outdoing one another. Some of them "did not speak to each other for years, so skilfully were their jealousies and rivalries played upon." [31]

If life at the managerial level in the Carnegie empire was not all sweet accord, the condition of the laborers in the mills was incredibly bad. "The lot of a skilled workman," said Andrew Carnegie, "is far better than that of the heir to an hereditary title, who is likely to lead an unhappy, wicked life." [32] But the Homestead workmen whom Hamlin Garland saw and talked to hardly bore out this pious judgment. "Everywhere in the enormous sheds were pits gaping like the mouth of hell, and ovens emitting a terrible degree of heat . . . one man jumps down, works desperately for a few minutes, and is then pulled up exhausted." Said one workman: "The worst part of the whole business is, it brutalizes a man. You can't help it . . . It's like any severe labor; it drags you down mentally and morally just as it does physically. I wouldn't mind it so much but for the long hours. Twelve hours is too long." [33] Work in Carnegie's steel mills was no worse than in any other. But neither was it any better. And it must have been difficult for a man with Carnegie's moral outlook to feel that the goal of making money justified the price being paid.

Meanwhile, however, the money was piling up; the Carnegie industrial empire was expanding at a fantastic rate. No matter what the cost, the god of the market place was being served. In 1887, the Carnegie profits were close to $3,500,000. In 1888, a stormy year in American industry, they dropped to less than $2,000,000. Thereafter, however, and especially after 1895, returns increased amazingly:

1889	$3,540,000	1895	$ 5,000,000
1890	5,350,000	1896	6,000,000
1891	4,300,000	1897	7,000,000
1892	4,000,000	1898	11,500,000
1893	3,000,000	1899	21,000,000
1894	4,000,000	plus $4,500,000 reinvested [34]

In 1900, the last year of Carnegie steel's independent existence, the profits reached the extraordinary total of $40,000,000. Meanwhile, production had, of course, risen proportionately. "In 1885, Great Britain led the world in the production of steel. Her total output for that year was 695,000 tons *less* than the product of the Carnegie Steel Company in 1899." [35]

It is difficult, without adopting a hortatory tone, to convey a picture of what these figures mean. They were the result not only of expanding industrial outlets and a favorable "tollgate" position, but of a single-minded pursuit of the main chance that left a trail of ruined competitors and

"partners" strewn in the wake. By the account of the com
pany officials themselves, this great expansion was in par
made possible by the complete victory scored over labor in
the bloody Homestead strike. The reëstablishment of th
twelve-hour day, which both Carnegie and his productio
chief Captain "Bill" Jones had condemned as backbreaking
helped too.[36] Finally, the introduction of speed-up methoc
under the guidance of Henry C. Frick increased both produc
tion and profits.

The contrast between this ruthless struggle for gain an
a personal philosophy of moral humanitarianism is cle
enough. But the immobilization of the latter ideal on occ
sions when the conflict occurred head-on is illustrated an
to a large degree, epitomized in the story of Homestead.

III

The tale begins with an article written by Carnegie
Forum Magazine in 1886 and subsequently republished
The Gospel of Wealth. The article was called "The Resu
of the Labor Struggle" and was mainly devoted to a revi
of the industrial strife that had alarmed the nation in
spring of 1886. The disturbances had evoked a chorus
dismay from the press, and suggestions to forestall th
recurrence had included a proposal to restrict the suffra
Carnegie scoffed at the forebodings expressed and rejec
all extremist solutions. "It will soon be seen," he said, "
what occurred was a very inadequate cause for the al
created. The eruption was not, in itself, a very serious r
ter, either in its extent or in its consequences. Its lesson
in the indications it gave of the forces underlying it." [37]

Carnegie then proceeded to draw certain morals f
the upheaval. Much of the trouble, he said, was causec
a trifle, and he implied that the intransigence of manager
had aggravated the situation unduly. "There is nothing

good for both parties to be derived from labor teaching the representative of capital the dignity of man, as man. The workingman, becoming more and more intelligent, will hereafter demand the treatment due to an equal." [38] Some of the trouble had arisen over the workers' demand for an eight-hour day. The immediate fulfillment of this aim Carnegie felt was impossible; but he acknowledged the justice of the eight-hour movement and suggested that it must eventually be successful. Finally, while condemning the violence that had flared in the heat of the conflict, he followed his condemnation with these eminently reasonable words:

I would have the public give due consideration to the terrible temptation to which the working-man on a strike is sometimes subjected. To expect that one dependent upon his daily wage for the necessaries of life will stand by peaceably and see a new man employed in his stead, is to expect much . . . the employer of labor will find it much more to his interest, wherever possible, to allow his works to remain idle and await the results of a dispute, than to employ the class of men that can be induced to take the place of other men who have stopped work. . . . There is an unwritten law among the best workmen: "Thou shalt not take thy neighbor's job." No wise employer will lightly lose his old employees. Length of service counts for much in many ways. Calling upon strange men should be the last resort.[39]

The article ended on the same conciliatory note: "Kept within legal limits," disputes between capital and labor are encouraging signs, "for they betoken the desire of the working-man to better his condition and upon this desire hang all hopes of advancement of the masses." Add now to these publicly stated and highly publicized views another statement which had appeared in *Forum* earlier in the same year: "The right of the working-men to combine and form trades-unions is no less sacred than the right of the manufacturer

to enter into associations and conferences with his fellows, and it must sooner or later be conceded. Indeed, it gives one but a poor opinion of the American workman if he permits himself to be deprived of a right which his fellow in England has long since conquered for himself. My experience has been that trades-unions, upon the whole, are beneficial both to labor and to capital." [40] These sentiments, expressed by the man who owned controlling interest in their plant, did not, of course, go unnoticed by Carnegie's employees. In fact, when a labor settlement was being negotiated in 1887, Carnegie handed each member of a workers' committee a reprint of his second *Forum* essay. Quite naturally, as Bridge remarks, "they mistook these high philanthropic views for the serious design of their employer towards themselves." [41]

Now to turn to Homestead. This plant had been operating for some time under the terms of a wage agreement with the Amalgamated Association of Iron and Steel Workers, the agreement being based on a tonnage rate set before certain technical advances in steel manufacturing had been made. The Carnegie management had found it increasingly difficult to deal with the Association but, partly on Carnegie's insistence, had made no effort to break the union. In 1892, however, it was determined that the tonnage scale must be adjusted downward, the contention being that wages were absorbing too large a share of the increased profits from technical improvements. At the same time, it seems to have been decided that the occasion was ripe for breaking the union itself, and Carnegie's full participation in these calculations is made clear by a notice he drafted in April and sent to Frick for posting in the Homestead plant. Among other things, this document announced that "these works, therefore, will be necessarily Non-Union after the expiration of the present agreement." [42] Frick, who was active manager at the time, declined to post the notice, but prepared nevertheless for the battle he knew was in the offing. Carnegie sailed for Europe, well aware of Frick's plans.

After a futile attempt to negotiate differences, Frick announced that he would close the Homestead works on July 1, 1892, and reopen on July 6 with whatever labor he could obtain. The workmen, still beguiled by Carnegie's public discourses, were convinced that Frick was bluffing; it was inconceivable to them that "the little boss" would permit the violation of the "unwritten law" of his *Forum* article. They organized on a makeshift military basis to repel invasion of the Homestead plant. But Frick was not bluffing. On the night of July 4, he sent three hundred Pinkerton "guards" in barges up the Monongahela River with the mission of protecting the plant and preparing the way for the introduction of nonunion workmen. The attempt was ill advised: the passage of the barges was observed, the workers mobilized to protect their jobs, and a battle ensued in which at least ten men were killed and over sixty wounded. The Pinkerton men were driven out, and the rule of the strikers in Homestead ended only on July 10, when the governor called out the National Guard.

Back in possession of the plant, Frick laid down terms of unconditional surrender. The strike continued under more peaceful conditions, so that now the suffering among the workmen took the less dramatic form of slow starvation. Public sympathy toward the workmen was strong, though by no means unanimous; but it was stimulated by repeated comparisons of Carnegie's published principles and the action of his company. On November 21, the Amalgamated Association admitted defeat and called off the strike; the bloodiest chapter in American industrial history finally came to an end. In 1932, Hendrick could say, "Not a union man has since entered the Carnegie works." [43]

Meanwhile Carnegie, the beneficiary of this conquest, was doing his best to hold himself incommunicado in a lodge on Loch Rannoch in Scotland. Volumes have been written, by Carnegie himself, by his apologists and critics, discussing the rights and wrongs of the Homestead strike and the degree of his own complicity. The significant thing about the evidence on these points is its ambiguity. Undoubtedly Carnegie left America knowing that serious trouble was brewing; undoubtedly he was backing Frick in the plan to break the union. It is probably true that had he been actively managing the affair, no effort would have been made to open the plant with outside labor, as he implies in his own account of what happened.[44] Nevertheless, there can be little question that the union-breaking policy, once embarked upon by Frick, received Carnegie's positive acquiescence in secret cables to the battleground.[45] Nor can his disclaimer of responsibility on the ground that he had retired from active management be taken seriously. His majority interest gave him full power of control whenever he might choose to exercise it, and the real reason for his inaction is clarified in the public statement he issued when the outcry was at its height: "I have implicit confidence in those who are managing the mills." [46]

At any rate, he was attacked unmercifully, and the impeachment of his motives cut him deeply. Said the St. Louis *Post-Dispatch*: "Three months ago Andrew Carnegie was a man to be envied. Today he is an object of mingled pity and contempt. In the estimation of nine-tenths of the thinking people on both sides of the ocean, he has not only given the lie to all his antecedents, but confessed himself a moral coward." [47] An "Ultra-Radical Journal" in England compared his "beautiful sentiments about the blessing of giving" to the Homestead record; the Glasgow Trades Council voted to add him to the roll of fame "along with the names of

Judas Iscariot and James Carey"; Keir Hardie was reported to have sent to the workers at Homestead one hundred pounds that Carnegie had contributed to his election campaign.[48] How much all this troubled Carnegie is revealed in a letter to his partners:

I am well and able to take an interest in the wonders we see. Shall see you all early after the New Year. Think I'm about ten years older than when with you last. Europe has rung with Homestead, Homestead, until we are all sick of the name, but it is all over now —— So once again Happy New Year to all. I wish someone would write me about your good self. I cannot believe you can be well.

Ever your Pard, A.C.[49]

In part, no doubt, the chagrin was caused by the damage to his public reputation. He yearned to be known as a good and kindly man, a benefactor of humanity, and he had assiduously fashioned such a picture of himself in the public mind. The revelation of the other side of his character hurt his pride. But it is hard to escape concluding that he realized the blame was in part deserved. When he defends his conduct he takes up his position on premises which conform well enough with the absolutist view of property rights entertained by men like Frick, but these premises are at variance with his own frequently expressed notions, and it may fairly be inferred that he knew it. Nevertheless, in spite of this realization, he was not so emancipated, so far in advance of his times, that he could let principle interfere with the real and tangible compulsions of his business interest. What looked to the outside world like simple hypocrisy was in fact the reflection of his own inner struggle, of a fundamental dichotomy in his standard of value.

In practice, during most of his life, Andrew Carnegie resolved this conflict as he did the Homestead affair, in favor of the philosophy of material gain. On paper, in his published

essays concerning modern problems, he faced the issue more
formally, and it is to a specific consideration of those preachments that we must turn in order to see how he rationalized
the system of "free enterprise" and his own share in its
development.

IV

Stated simply, Carnegie's main concern in his writings
was the reconciliation of the capitalist order, which had made
him wealthy and famous, with the concept of moral value
inherited from his youth. He felt called upon, that is, to make
a case not only for capitalism but for democracy, since a
justification of both was essential to his own peace of mind.
The tendency of his arguments may therefore be summarized
in two general propositions. In the first place, he argued that
the American democratic system was largely responsible for
the remarkable progress of the Republic during the first century of its history. This is the leitmotiv of *Triumphant Democracy*, a paean of praise to America and all it has wrought.
Since, however, the most convincing sections of the book are
the accounts of material progress drawn from the census re-
ports, and since the case for a democracy can hardly be said
to be settled by the discovery that her cereal crop loaded on
freight cars will reach twice around the globe, Carnegie set
it forth as a second article of faith that all this material advance exists for no other purpose and tends to no other end
but to serve the spiritual welfare of the whole nation, in short,
to make men free. Thus a rounded system is developed:
democracy serves the purposes of capitalism; and capitalism
fructifies democracy.

Triumphant Democracy is on all counts an amazing book.
Sinclair Lewis was not to satirize the American philosophy of
boosterism for another forty years; yet here, in 1886, the high-
water mark of the doctrine is set by an immigrant Scot. It

might be George Babbitt himself who speaks in the preface to the 1893 edition: "There are, in my opinion, too many, Britons and Americans, whose chief mission in life and keenest delight seems to be to croak about, disparage, abuse, and even libel their respective countries." [50] For 549 pages thereafter, Carnegie proceeds to document all the charges of materialism and smug self-satisfaction which foreign critics have traditionally leveled at America.

Most of the volume is a recital of the industrial and material achievements of the nation. With respect to agriculture, it seems that "Ceres is indeed the prime divinity of the Republic." [51] America leads the world in the value of agricultural produce. The high percentage of farm mortgages are "evidence of his [the debtor's] enterprise and desire to obtain more land which was bound to increase in value." [52] So great is the American agricultural capacity that the future will probably find a larger and larger proportion of Europe dependent upon it. In field after field of manufacturing, America is passing the older countries, because the fathers of the Republic wisely planned for a variegated industrial system. In one decade manufacturing production has nearly doubled. This is due partly to the corps of technically trained young men produced by American schools, partly to a high respect for the dignity of labor, which makes American workmen the most efficient on earth.[53] In mineral wealth the American endowment is the greatest in the world.[54] America's gains in both foreign and domestic commerce have been terrific, but the domestic potential is so much the greater that the nation is self-contained, invulnerable to foreign threats should they arise.[55] The high tariff criticized by foreigners is no real deterrent to trade, because competition within the nation has established such low prices that the consumer "cannot be made to trouble himself very greatly with the question of the tariff." [56] Both American railways and waterways are superior to those of any other nation. Wages are higher than in any other land, and the relative price of goods to the workman is lower.[57]

"Not omitting aspects of more spiritual import," as a biographer says,[58] Carnegie turns to examine such matters as education, religion, and art. Again quantity is the index of value. One out of every five inhabitants attends the public schools; American millionaires have endowed "a remarkable list of educational institutions." [59] Eighteen millions of Americans are churchgoers. As for art, "the New World has been steadily transferring to the galleries of its collectors the greatest paintings produced by . . . the most famous school of artists of the century." [60] "Our architecture is strong, fruitful, ever increasing in beauty and richness." [61]

What are the factors that account for this astonishing record of accomplishment and progress? They are, says Carnegie, three: "the ethnic character of the people, the topographical and climatic conditions under which they developed, and the influence of political institutions founded upon the equality of the citizen." [62] The first reason need not delay us. Carnegie was inordinately proud of his Scottish origin and accepted the current dicta of more learned men than he regarding the innate superiority of the Northern European. The second causal factor is too obvious for comment. But the real message of the book is contained in the eulogy of democracy. Besides extolling the virtues of his adopted land, Carnegie was also trying, in *Triumphant Democracy*, to draw an object lesson for Great Britain. The acceptance of American democratic institutions by the mother country was the necessary first step to realization of his lifelong dream — federal union between the United States and Great Britain.

Carnegie labors hard to establish a causal link between democracy and progress, but in the end it rests on an act of faith. He sometimes seems to argue that the triumphant

American advance was made possible by the abolition of hereditary privilege; but of course the medieval privileges which still survived in England at the time of his writing were hardly worth mentioning. Carnegie meant something more than that democracy had removed the economic barriers to free trade that were the heritage of feudalism. He had always felt a deep sense of degradation because Britain denied to him the rights of first-class citizenship.[63] The participation of all the people in political decisions was, he argued, an essential ingredient of social justice.[64] Then, since he believed in the moral rightness of political equality, he also felt compelled to believe in its beneficence. He therefore advanced the proposition that the removal of the taint of political inferiority sets free the best instincts of man and leads to the attainment of the millennium.[65] Only a politically emancipated people could have fashioned the miracle of America.

Two points in particular are worth making about this book and its argument. In the first place, it is noteworthy that Carnegie defines democratic equality strictly in political terms as the freedom of the ballot box, and privilege as that species of preferment which rests on hereditary caste distinctions. He was using without change the political frame of reference he had inherited from his Chartist forefathers, which had at best a limited relevance to the problems of 1890 in either Britain or America. His advocacy of democratic institutions, then, amounted to little more than a stout espousal of forms everyone was in favor of already. Inequality and privilege arising from the nature of the economic system were, for the time, overlooked; the tendency of political democracy to degenerate into plutocracy was disregarded. In the second place, he comes narrowly close, in *Triumphant Democracy*, to identifying the aims of democracy with the aims of capitalism. By the nature and quantity of his examples, he seems to be saying that democracy is justified by the railroads it builds and the wheat it produces. Other implications can be found, it is true.[66] But the more pervasive suggestion and the inference that readers like Spencer and Arnold drew was that democratic objectives and material progress were nearly synonymous.

With these two premises assumed, Carnegie could go on to glorify the Republic without reservation. It would be idle to rehearse his eulogies of American political institutions — federalism, the House and the Senate, the Supreme Court, the Presidency. All are treated as perfect, and the commentary simply echoes the tune of thousands of Fourth of July orations. This institutional superiority is both defined and accounted for by a single fact — the absence of a hereditary ruling class;[67] and this fact has opened the way to a period of development that posterity will regard as the golden age.[68]

It would be simple to dismiss *Triumphant Democracy* as merely a naïve and willfully uncritical panegyric to America in the age of enterprise. It deserves these strictures, of course. But the important question for one who would understand Carnegie is not so much the message of the book as its motive. Why did he bother to write it at all? Why should one of the wealthiest and most powerful of American industrialists feel driven to write such a book as this, a book whose subject matter is so foreign to his own field of special competence? The answer to the question reveals a good deal about Carnegie. It seems reasonable to believe that he wrote *Triumphant Democracy* because he had an imperious need to explain and justify himself and his environment, because he had to convince both the world and himself that what he was doing was good and that the context within which he operated was just. The book appears to be a defense of democracy; actually, it is a defense of nineteenth-century capitalism — and Carnegie. That is why capitalism and democracy keep getting mixed up, why the meaning of democratic equality is so sharply limited (to accord with approximate contemporary realities), why material welfare is treated as a universal good. Carnegie is trying, whether he knows it or not, to frame a reply to that private memorandum he wrote in 1868, to answer the voice of his conscience which warned that the pursuit of wealth would ultimately degrade him.

But in spite of the fatuously optimistic tone of *Triumphant Democracy*, or rather because of it, there is a feeling that he protests too much. His assurance that "all is well, since all grows better" has a hollow ring, and it may well be doubted that he fully believed in his own vision of perfection. The fallacy of the two major assumptions was too obvious to be really ignored, especially by a man who, like Carnegie, had some appreciation of humanistic and aesthetic values. He never clearly repudiated the simple identification of capitalist and democratic aims which is the theme of *Triumphant Democracy*. That the measure of a society's goodness is its capital accumulation was essentially Sumner's conclusion, and there were times when Carnegie seemed to affirm it. But at other times he appeared to feel the need for something more. He accepted the main outlines of the contemporary capitalist environment; but he was impelled to go a step beyond either Sumner or Field in finding his justification for it. He had to explain to his conscience that "free enterprise" capitalism was not only materially productive, as Sumner claimed, not only divinely decreed, as Field insisted, but also destined to produce a better and happier world.

This search for a rationale is the dominant concern of Carnegie's other writings on political and social questions, and the solution of the conservative-democratic dilemma which he develops depends upon two major lines of approach. For one thing, Carnegie adopts an evolutionary concept of social progress, derived largely from Spencer, but revised and simplified to suit his own intellectual and emotional needs. In the second place, he evolves the idea of business trusteeship as the moral obligation of men of wealth. On these two cornerstones he rests his case.

Carnegie's acceptance of the idea of evolutionary progress meant more to him than the resolution of religious uncertainties. The analogy between the progressive development of organic species and the improvement of man's social condition appealed to his native optimistic bias; but more important, it provided him with a moral framework in which he and capitalism might find their appointed place. His evolutionism was completely sanguine. Although he corresponded with Spencer until the end and called him "Master," he never shared the pessimism that beset that messiah in later life. "The evolutionist," said Carnegie, "who sees nothing but certain and steady progress for the race will never attempt to set bounds to its triumphs, even to its final form of complete and universal industrial cooperation." "The evolutionist has never any doubt about the realization of the highest ideals from the operation of that tendency within us, not ourselves, which makes for righteousness." [69]

But the acceptance of the evolutionary hypothesis implies more than a glowing future for humanity. It also suggests, or suggested to Carnegie, that the present is a necessary improvement on the past, that the capitalist order with its regime of economic freedom marks an advance over previous epochs when individual enterprise was artificially restrained. "The progress of man from the earliest day up to the present has been one steady march upward . . . when we in our enlightened age know that man is an outgrowth from lower orders of life, and has implanted within him the instinct which compels him to turn his face to the sun and slowly move upward toward that which is better, rejecting in his progress

after test, all that injures or debases, the call upon us by our
Socialist friends to exchange the individualistic civilized present which we have reached after many hundreds of thousands of years of progress, for the system of communism of
the savage past is indeed startling." [70] Thus the analogy of
evolution not only guarantees the future but assures us that
the present is better than the past.

Finally, evolutionism precludes any sudden changes in
the existing order. "Man's progress in the past has been steady
and he has travelled upward from savagery, but long is the
road and devious the way to complete change of the organic
structure of the economic and personal relationships of modern society. . . We have before us the work of our own day
and generation, and only this can we push forward during our
lives." [71] This last reservation might be thought to qualify
Carnegie's optimism, as indeed in strict logic it probably does,
but the qualification is obscured by the rosy assumption that
man's state is already the most felicitous that history records.

Armed with these three deductions from his concept of
social evolution, Carnegie turns to an analysis of current problems. It can be seen now that the nineteenth-century American capitalist system, both in its virtues and its seeming
flaws, is justified as a necessary step in human progress. Economic individualism, the acquisitive instinct, is ultimately
benign in spite of the incidental harshness of its operation.
The competition of human beings, each attempting to improve his own lot at the expense of his fellows, has given rise
to "our wonderful material development, which brings im-
proved conditions in its train." [72] This is true because under
individualism exceptional persons "are left in perfect freedom
and in the possession of glorious liberty of choice, free 'by the
sole act of their own unlorded will' to obey the Divine call
which consecrates each to his great mission." [73] Individualism,
by the same reasoning, is the key to man's future. "Not uni-

formity but infinite diversity, ensured this progress, and as far as we can see, it is through diversity alone that the race can continue its upward march. The exceptional man in every department must be permitted and encouraged to develop his unusual powers, tastes and ambitions in accordance with the laws [the survival of the fittest] which prevail in everything that lives or grows." [74] And even if we wished to substitute an unselfish ideal for individualism, even if we wished to establish the good society upon another base, we could not do so in the foreseeable future, for such a change would involve an alteration in human nature; "this is not evolution, but revolution." [75]

It goes without saying, then, that private property must be protected, for "upon the sacredness of property civilization itself depends." [76] For capital is the precondition of civilization, and capital is accumulated most effectively when the individual labors to amass it on his own behalf. Individualism and private property, which are sanctified by the immutable law of human development, have given us unexampled well-being already and may be expected to do even better later on. [77]

But there persist, even in the lap of this bounty, a few apparent injustices. Industrial society seems to have fostered, for example, great inequalities in economic circumstance and to have produced great aggregations of wealth, which threaten to hamper the workings of the evolutionary laws. But, in response to such criticism, it should be noted that the accumulation of wealth in the hands of a few is not only the main source of our present felicity, but the precondition of the bright new world of the future. "We accept and welcome, therefore, as conditions to which we must accommodate ourselves, great inequality of environment; the concentration of business, industrial and commercial, in the hands of a few; and the law of competition between these as being not only

beneficial, but essential to the future progress of the race." [78]
Men who have acquired wealth must not be disturbed during
their life, because "millions honestly made in any useful occupation give evidence of ability, foresight and assiduity above
the common, and prove the man who has made them a very
valuable member of society." [79] Moreover, poverty, the extent
of which is greatly exaggerated, is a blessing in any case to its
happy possessor. "To be born to honest poverty and compelled to labor and strive for a livelihood in youth is the best
of all schools for developing latent qualities, strengthening
character, and making useful men." [80] "I heartily subscribe to
President Garfield's doctrine that 'the richest heritage a
young man can be born to is poverty.'" [81] As for the aggregations of wealth which are called "trusts," insofar as they are
simply large concentrations of capital, they benefit the nation
by facilitating the cheaper production of more commodities.
Any attempt by them to monopolize production and raise
prices artificially is foredoomed to failure under the iron law
of competition.[82]

Now Carnegie's justification of the regime of "free enterprise" was of course far from unique. And it would appear,
with no further emendation, to furnish him with precisely the
self-justification he was seeking. Carnegie could then be set
down as differing from Sumner only in that he was more in-
clined to slur over the harsh features of modern industrial
society, more hopeful about the millennium which capitalism
would inaugurate. If he really believed in the philosophy of
unrestrained economic competition, nothing more need have
been said.

But the trouble was that, even with the support of the
great body of American public opinion in his generation, even
with the assurances of the Spencerian revelation and the dogmas of orthodox economics, he was never quite satisfied. He
pretended to take the same unflinching attitude toward the

iron law of self-help and competition that men like Sumner
and Spencer had adopted; like them he even condemned private charity as a sin against society.[83] But he could not rid
himself of the feeling that a man who lived with no other
thought than his own selfish gain was somehow ignoble; in
spite of his own protestations, the idea that such a man is the
modern social hero and willy-nilly the benefactor of the community was ultimately unconvincing. The inequality of
wealth which he hailed as wholly benign in one breath, he
appeared to deplore in the next as "one of the crying evils of
our day." [84] On the other hand, since his thinking reflected an
effort to justify his own life, he had to accept a large part of
the Sumnerian gospel. He had devoted himself to the pursui
of material gain, driven by an impulsion he could not resist
and in hewing his path to success he cut down competitor
with ruthless abandon, he built a fortune on sweated labo
It was essential for him to believe that this course of actic
was ethically warranted, that the laws of Accumulation
Wealth and Competition by which he had lived were ul
mately benevolent.

What he did, therefore, was to accept the contempora
capitalist rationale up to a point without qualification.
view of the present state of human nature, an economic or
based on individual self-seeking is the best that can be
vised, since it places the economic tools of the communit
the hands of those best fitted to use them. Any impor
modification of this rule — that the fit must be allowe
accumulate the lion's share of available capital — would
irreparable harm to society and delay the onward mar
civilization.

This decided, however, he would go no farther. He
not and could not swallow the doctrine that, in usir
wealth, the capitalist owed the community no obligatic
acquiring his millions, the captain of industry must be

by the standing rules of self-service and dog eat dog. But having achieved wealth, he cannot thereafter regard it as a private possession with no strings attached; he must consider himself "a trustee for the poor, intrusted for a season with a great part of the increased wealth of the community, but administering it for the community far better than it could or would have done for itself." [85]

This idea of business trusteeship is of course the most distinctive feature of Carnegie's thought, and it merits careful examination. To begin with, although the term is sometimes used as if it had a more general application, its effective meaning for Carnegie is fairly specific and limited. It does not mean that in his practical business operations the capitalist must subordinate his own self-interest to the welfare of the community, for such an implication would obviously be incompatible with the individualist principles to which Carnegie has already subscribed. He does argue that the man who enjoys a surplus of wealth is forced by simple necessity to use that surplus in a way that benefits the public; he can personally consume only a limited amount; the remainder must be reinvested, thus promoting community welfare by increasing the aggregate capital stock. [86] But this is merely a beneficent accident. The businessman serves the world best by seeking to serve himself. In the actual pursuit of wealth, the rule of self-aggrandizement still prevails.

If Carnegie is held to the logic of his premises, the concrete social duty involved in the concept of trusteeship amounts simply to this: that the man who has been clever and fortunate enough to acquire wealth must, at some point in his life, cease to "gather honey," in Carnegie's characteristic phrase, and devote himself thereafter to the task of redistributing his millions in a way that will benefit all. [87] Carnegie's assertion of this capitalist imperative is based on the following reasoning. The wealth of the successful businessman is a

product of two factors: his own foresight, resourcefulness, and thrift; and the general increase in population and values in the community.[88] Since the millionaire has by definition unmistakably demonstrated that he is the man best equipped to draw the maximum utility from the social potential, he should not be restricted in his performance of that function while he lives.[89] But when he dies the situation is quite different. His heirs have given no such evidence of their fitness to control the community's capital assets; moreover, the inheritance of wealth is a curse, not a blessing. Therefore, if a man dies rich, a very large portion of his wealth should be taken by the state.[90]

But for the millionaire who fulfills his social duty this eventuality need never and should never present itself. For "the man who dies thus rich dies disgraced."[91] His real task is to distribute his money usefully before he dies — not in the form of charity, but in forms which will "stimulate the best and most aspiring poor of the community to further efforts for their own improvement."[92] And this should be done by the millionaire himself *before* his death so that "his poorer brethren" will have the benefit of "his superior wisdom, experience, and ability to administer."[93]

There are a number of observations, both appreciative and critical, that could be made about this concept. When we consider that the doctrine originated in the mind of one of America's greatest multimillionaires at a time when most of his fellows were maintaining that wealth justifies itself, and when we consider that Carnegie put his theory into practice by giving away most of his millions, we can hardly begrudge him some credit and admiration. But such reflections should not obscure an understanding of the real character of Carnegie's thought. The gospel of trusteeship was important to Carnegie because it enabled him to justify the "free enterprise" world which had made him rich and famous, and to crown the multimillionaire in that society (i.e., himself) with the garland of social heroism.

The elitist implication of the idea that the millionaire must distribute his wealth during his own lifetime is unmistakable. He is, by hypothesis, best qualified to judge what measures will serve the welfare of the community. Not only is he the "fittest" in the economic arena, he is also the proper custodian of society's future; he is no mere profit-taker, but a social planner endowed with more insight and wisdom than the state itself can possibly achieve. So the last lingering taint of ignobility is erased from the concept of entrepreneurship. Carnegie's and America's instinct to canonize the successful businessman is provided with a rationale. The function of social as well as economic leadership falls naturally to the lot of the captain of industry.

Moreover, with the development of the concept of trusteeship, the last bar to evolutionary progress under capitalism is removed and a philosophy of optimism is conclusively vindicated. It is true that the steady improvement and diffusion of welfare is ultimately inevitable in any case. But the great trouble with such a doctrine of evolutionary advance is that the millennium is postponed while the iron laws take their tardy course. In the immediate future the prospect is for a continuation of present class friction and dissatisfaction, a prolongation of human misery and vice. With the ideal of trusteeship to guide its appointed leaders, however, society can anticipate a much accelerated rate of progress; in fact, the problem of rich and poor will soon be solved.[94]

Finally, and most important of all, the trusteeship doctrine forges the last link in the chain which binds capitalism and democracy. It justifies a life largely devoted to pecuniary striving; it rationalizes the preoccupation with materialist ideals. Democratic and humane values are the ends; economic individualism is the means. The divided moral personality which is characteristic of both Carnegie and the age he lived in is provided with an escape from its impasse, an escape which allows the individual to surrender to materialist compulsions while comforting himself with the assurance that in so doing he serves a nobler end. The hard empirical ethic of Sumner is given its final gloss and, without seeming to, achieves its final triumph.

For with this junction of capitalism and democracy in an inseparable means-ends alliance, the last barrier to the apostasy of democratic idealism is surmounted. Sumner might urge the frank espousal of a social norm based on material utility; Stephen Field might argue in effect that democratic freedom and economic freedom are one. To not a few Americans in the age of enterprise these arguments were persuasive enough to stand alone; they closed out the case for conservatism. But in the minds of others some vagrant doubts survived, an intimation persisted that liberty in the economic sense and liberty in the democratic sense might not be quite identical. To these somewhat more reluctant devotees of the conservative faith a rationale like Carnegie's supplied the answer. Inhibit economic liberty and democracy must suffer, as surely as it will thrive if capitalist energies are given free scope. Capitalism and democracy may not be identical; but they cannot be disjoined. The one is the soil in which the other flourishes; they are related as cause to effect. The distinction between an end in itself and a necessary means to that end is too subtle to endure: the ground swell of popular thought tends to obliterate such nice discriminations. Conservatism could now absorb democracy. The American tradition could lose itself in the sterile pursuit of a materialist ideal.

seven

CONCLUSIONS

I

The conservative credo which is the subject of these essays has been exposed to some savage onslaughts since the halcyon days of its greatest prestige. The very men who helped formulate the doctrine and undertook to provide it with a popular exegesis — men like Sumner and Carnegie and Field — lived to see it challenged sharply by public opinion; and as the twentieth century has worn on, the scattered expressions of discontent have swelled at times to a full chorus. On all fronts the proponents of naïve capitalism have beaten a slow retreat; one by one the outlying citadels of Sumnerism have fallen. If destiny had a sense of humor, Sumner would surely have been preserved to see what use Franklin Roosevelt made of his phrase, "the forgotten man."

But if nineteenth-century conservatism has encountered setbacks in the troubled milieu of the twentieth, it has by no means surrendered the field. Its vitality has endured two world wars and the profoundest economic depression in history, and in essential respects the dogma remains robust enough to lay a potent claim to the homage of the nation. Each proposal to curtail economic liberty by legislation must still make its way against the presumption of un-Americanism; any basic departure from the pattern of "free enterprise" is still widely regarded as an inroad on democracy. The leaders of public policy ignore this American folk belief at their peril. In this study an effort has been made to analyze the process by which conservatism attained this powerful ideological position, and it may be well, before concluding, to gather together the main strands of the analysis.

I have suggested that the new world which dawned after Appomattox ushered in not only a radical alteration in the economic and social structure of American life, but a fundamental revision of the democratic tradition. Post-bellum political thought was distinguished by two salient and related characteristics — its materialist premises and its conservative conclusions. And if the relationship between them is not one of direct cause and effect, at least it is clear that the juxtaposition of these qualities in the American mind is more than a casual coincidence. Materialism nourished conservatism and helped to sustain it by enabling conservative spokesmen to draw on the resources of strength contained in the ideals of democracy.

Let me be clear about the argument on this point. I do not suggest that men like Sumner and Field would have been liberal democrats on the Jeffersonian model if their value system had been less clearly oriented toward materialism. They would have been conservatives in any age, ranging themselves, in Fisher Ames's terms, on the side of "the wise, the rich, and the good." But I do suggest that this value system, which they shared with the bulk of their countrymen, helped to determine the special character of the conservative rationale they espoused. Much that was warm and humanistic in the older tory tradition was swept aside in deference to a cold and sometimes brutal calculus of utility. I suggest also that the devotion to a material ideal which characterizes the thinking of these men helped to exaggerate the extent of their conservatism by releasing it from the inhibitions a different norm might have imposed. It left them free to follow out the logical implications of their postulates. And, finally, I suggest that the adoption of this ideal by the nation at large made it possible for conservatism to remold the democratic faith, to infuse its catchwords with entrepreneurial meanings, and, most important of all, to retail the synthesis under the guise of traditional democracy.

The social theory of William Graham Sumner is by and large the clearest and most uncompromising exposition of Gilded Age conservative doctrine that the literature of the time affords. It is in Sumner that we can trace most faithfully both the source and the issue of the nineteenth-century capitalist rationale; he was, as Ward saw, not only its firmest ally but its most dangerous friend. For in Sumner the premises are stripped of adornment, their implications are accepted unflinchingly, the arid wasteland of moral materialism is exposed.

Sumner's thinking derived in its main outlines from the coupling of a deep-rooted Protestant ideal of virtuous conduct with an instinctive empirical bias. Gradually, as a naïve concept of the scientific attitude gained dominance over his mind, the spiritual bases of his moral attitudes were sloughed away, so that he was led to seek justification for that morality in the only realm of being whose authority he could recognize — the world of concrete fact. Having convinced himself that the intangible is the nonexistent, and being unable either by temperament or training to dispense altogether with the idea of right and wrong, he naturally adopted a social ethic grounded in material utility; and the case he made for "free enterprise" was based throughout on this central value judgment.

The validity of this norm being assumed, his argument could proceed. The abracadabras of Social Darwinism and of orthodox economics were employed to support the claim of capitalism to construct a political order on its own terms. All the old objectives of American conservatism were strengthened and restated. The ethic of material utility led first to the conclusion that capital accumulation is synonymous with social advance; thence, with the help of the Darwinian analogy, we are led to concede that the only genuinely moral instinct is acquisitiveness, that the good man is he who pursues material gain most assiduously, and that he has social value in proportion as his efforts are rewarded by success.

Thus with a few strokes of the pen the basis was laid for a reaffirmation of the sanctity of property; and the claim of the select few to govern the most essential aspects of community existence was asserted and proved. The democratic principle of popular rule is seen on this reasoning to be fatuous nonsense. Under the best possible management, external interference with the natural process of struggle and selection is certain to call forth unforeseen reactions which may well divert the social mechanism from its proper course. But if the results of social tinkering are always likely to be pernicious, in a democratic state the probability becomes a certainty. For democracy implies that political decision-making is delegated to those most poorly qualified to discharge the function. Even worse, under popular control the tendency of all states to degenerate into instruments of class aggrandizement is greatly enhanced. The only solution is to exclude the state from the process of social decision altogether, to hedge the majority about with limitations in the hope they will be effective to save society from itself. And the first step toward that objective involves a redefinition of such useful but presently meaningless concepts as Justice and Liberty. Let "right" become the right to keep what we earn and use it as we will; let "equality" become legally protected inequality; and the chances are at least fair that society will continue its upward march.

This was Sumnerism and these were, in essence, the conservative arguments that clamored for acceptance as the Gilded Age advanced. There is a sort of impressive logic about the way each tenet of Sumnerism moved to take its place in American mores and governmental institutions. The Supreme Court undertook, with public acquiescence, the vast job of reshaping the constitutional structure. Point by point, having accepted Sumner's central premise, the justices were driven to implement his conclusions. In amended but still recognizable form, the constitutional doctrine of the *Lochner* case is the social theory of *The Challenge of Facts*. The academic superstructure has been replaced by a network of legalism which somewhat obscures but cannot conceal the fact that in root and issue the two philosophies were identical.

In Stephen Field we can observe the logic of this conservatism at close range; we can trace the corrosion of a personal value system; we can move closer to an understanding of the nineteenth-century version of democracy. Poles apart from Sumner in his terminology and methods, Field moved nevertheless in the same conservative mainstream. He embraced the materialist value postulate that Sumner laid down, but translated his conclusions into language more consonant with the American tradition. The relativistic and "scientific" Sumnerian concept of right became, in Field's opinions, an absolute. Where Sumner recognized the need for a revision of democratic ideas of liberty and equality, Field showed how the metamorphosis could be accomplished. While purporting to reconfirm the democratic tradition, he transfigured it. And in his own thinking the end result of such a corruption in American social values is revealed: from being merely predominant in his hierarchy of ideals, the property right becomes in time an exclusive concern.

The restatement of Sumnerian conservatism which must take place before the restatement of democracy can be effective becomes more nearly complete in the formulations of

Andrew Carnegie, and at the same time the value conflicts that plagued the Gilded Age are given dramatic illustration. The rank materialism and implied pessimism of the basic creed are glossed over and obscured. The aims of humanitarian democracy are not abjured; their realization is merely postponed until the benign laws of accumulation of wealth and competition can prepare the ground. Democracy's subservience to capitalism is concealed on the pretext that, in the long run, capitalism will serve democracy. Meanwhile, the heroism of the successful entrepreneur, which Sumner asserted and Field assumed, is confirmed and given a new justification. The infallible evidence of success itself should be enough to establish the natural superiority and social value of the businessman. But the stubborn American public which still confusedly persists in looking for feet of clay must be confronted with overwhelming evidence that the search is a vain one. The Western tradition that a moral act involves a moral intent must somehow be appeased. The answer is the theory of trusteeship — the doctrine that the man who has proved his superiority by success in the economic struggle is the custodian of the community's substance, that he rightfully acquires and controls great wealth, but that he must renounce his stewardship before death and remit his accumulation to the community, its residual owner. The means employed in the pursuit of wealth are thus absolved of taint because of the basically moral purpose that underlies them; and the competitive order — "free enterprise" — can go its way, still hallowed and still undisturbed.

II

Nineteenth-century conservatism, like most living things, had begun to die a little even before it had fully matured. In essence it consisted not of "laissez faire," not of "free enterprise," not even of "rugged individualism," but rather of an attempt to define good and right as that which the economic man does to achieve success. And an ideology which so exalts material accomplishment must ultimately prove itself by the same standard. Since "laissez faire" capitalism failed in various respects to fulfill its own implied promises, the American people tended to exact the just price for those failures, and public policy moved farther and farther from the world of autonomous business enterprise championed by William Sumner.

Carnegie indeed foresaw this development, and there is a sense, not emphasized by this study, in which he can be described as standing at the crossroads of American conservative thinking. Behind him and still dominant in his syndrome of drives and values is the root-hog-or-die theory of capitalist enterprise with which these essays are concerned. Ahead and partly anticipated by him is a conservative rationale that focuses on the positive social duty of business entrepreneurship. Carnegie had begun to see what modern businessmen are recognizing with increasing certainty — that "free enterprise" must, in the last analysis, be justified by its works.

If it can be justified, no one can find cause to quarrel with it. But it seems fair to ask that the issue be plain. And the cause of clarity is not served by perpetuating a myth which identifies an unregulated economic order with democracy. That notion was the result, as we have seen, of a corrosion of national ideals so pervasive that it apostatized the American political tradition. In one form or another, the confusions thus inaugurated have survived to clog the channels of public policy ever since. Democracy, however, is condemned to no such misalliance. Economic regulation of business enterprise raises grave issues, but no question of the betrayal of democracy is involved. The master concern of democracy in America is not business but humanity; and the problem of social control should be judged with that truth in mind.

NOTES

TABLE OF CASES

INDEX

NOTES

CHAPTER ONE. CONSERVATISM AND DEMOCRACY

1. Slaughter-House Cases, 16 Wallace 36 (1873).
2. Edwin Mims, *The Majority of the People* (New York, 1941), pp. 213–221.
3. Carl Becker, *The Declaration of Independence* (New York, 1942), p. 278.
4. Walter Lippmann, *Men of Destiny* (New York, 1927), pp. 49–55.
5. Karl Marx and Friedrich Engels, "The Communist Manifesto," in Emile Burns, *Handbook of Marxism* (New York, 1935), p. 25.
6. "There were plenty of scientific bigots who would have liked to annihilate what they could not weigh. Certainly it is true that the general effect of science at first was to create impatience with the emotional life. Many proud possessors of the Spencerian mind devoted their glowing youth to a study of those bleak books which used to pass for scientific manuals. They regarded religion with scorn and art with condescension, and sometimes they nerved themselves up to admire beauty as one of the necessary weaknesses of an otherwise reasonable man. Truth for them was as neat as a checkerboard, and they made you feel like the man from Corinth who asked a Spartan 'whether trees grew square in his country'" (Walter Lippmann, *Drift and Mastery* [New York, 1914], pp. 291–292).
7. H. S. Churchill, *The City Is the People* (New York, 1945), p. 22.
8. R. H. Gabriel, *The Course of American Democratic Thought* (New York, 1940), p. 150.
9. Rudyard Kipling, *American Notes* (New York, n.d.), p. 82. Said Van Wyck Brooks: "Money and 'numbers' governed all their thoughts, even and even especially, in the sphere of religion. For who could imagine a greater contrast than that between Moody and Beecher and the great religious leaders of the previous age, Theodore Parker and Channing" (*New England: Indian Summer* [New York, 1940], p. 98).
10. "In some strange way the intoxication which accompanied the acquisition of wealth affected those who had not, as well as those who had. The psychology of business not only clouded the judgment of the entrepreneurs and financiers; it also threatened to become a national way of thinking . . . the acquisitive instinct was glorified until it was regarded as a beneficent deity, devoted to the greater good of the country and not unworthy of the worship it received" (C. C. Regier, *The Era of the Muckrakers* [Chapel Hill, 1932], pp. 5–6).

11. C. A. Beard and M. R. Beard, *The American Spirit* (New York, 1942), pp. 341–342.

12. H. G. Wells in *The Future in America* (New York, 1906), p. 31, quotes a magazine article by Edgar Saltus, who preached a sermon on progress, drawing his inspiration from the Flatiron Building: "Evolution has not halted . . . it achieved an unrecognized advance when it devised buildings such as this. . . It will be demonstrable that, as buildings ascend, so do ideas. It is mental progress that skyscrapers engender."

13. Allen Nevins, *The Emergence of Modern America* (New York, 1927), pp. 89–90.

14. Said E. L. Godkin: "All being corrupt together, what is the use in our 'investigating' each other?" (*Nation*, May 22, 1873, p. 349). And young Henry Adams, viewing the gold scandal in 1869, said: "The worst scandals of the eighteenth century were relatively harmless by the side of this, which smirched executive, judiciary, banks, corporate systems, professions and people, all the great active forces of society in one dirty cesspool of vulgar corruption" (*The Education of Henry Adams* [New York: Modern Library, 1931], pp. 271–272).

15. As recent studies are showing, the pre-Sumter attitude was not nearly so hostile to government intervention in economic life as has usually been assumed. See Louis Hartz, *Economic Policy and Democratic Thought* (Cambridge: Harvard University Press, 1948), pt. IV.

16. Civil Rights Cases, 109 U.S. 3 (1883).

17. Pollock v. Farmers' Loan and Trust Co., 158 U.S. 601 (1895).

18. C. B. Swisher, *Stephen J. Field* (Washington, 1930), p. 247.

19. See Thorstein Veblen, *The Theory of the Leisure Class* (New York: Modern Library, 1934), and *The Instinct of Workmanship* (New York, 1946).

20. V. L. Parrington, *Main Currents in American Thought*, 3 vols. (New York, 1927–1930), III, 409.

CHAPTER TWO. THE WORLD OF WILLIAM GRAHAM SUMNER

1. Most illuminating in this regard are the debates in the state constitutional conventions from about 1820 to 1850. See B. F. Wright, Jr., *American Interpretations of Natural Law* (Cambridge: Harvard University Press, 1931), pp. 182–210.

2. See Hamilton's "Report on Manufactures," *American State Papers: Finance*, I, 123–144.

3. "The road for the advance of industrial capitalism was opened up during the years of the Civil War and the Reconstruction periods; for it was during 1861–1875 . . . that the nation was committed fully to the protective system, a national banking structure, homesteads,

government aid to Pacific railways. . . By 1875, virtually, the task was done; and it remained merely for later politicians (Republicans, and, indeed, eastern Democrats) to act in the capacity of the train-wrecking crew in order to keep the tracks free of obstructions" (Louis M. Hacker, *The Triumph of American Capitalism* [New York, 1940], p. 383).

4.   See Joseph Dorfman, *The Economic Mind in American Civilization*, 2 vols. (New York, 1946), vol. II.

5.   Thorstein Veblen, *The Place of Science in Modern Civilization* (New York, 1919), p. 151.

6.   See Richard Hofstadter, *Social Darwinism in American Thought, 1860–1915* (Philadelphia, 1945), chap. 1. The literature on the subject is, of course, voluminous; even the novels of the period were often saturated with Spencerism (H. S. Commager, *The American Mind* [New Haven, 1950], chap. 6).

7.   *Education of Henry Adams*, p. 225.

8.   Fiske was Spencer's American high priest, while E. L. Youmans "became the self-appointed salesman of the scientific world outlook" (Hofstadter, *Social Darwinism*, p. 2).

9.   L. H. Morgan, *Ancient Society* (New York, 1877), p. 552.

10.   L. F. Ward, *Dynamic Sociology* (New York, 1883).

11.   W. L. Phelps, "When Yale Was Given to Sumnerology," *Literary Digest International Book Review*, III (1925), 661–663. H. E. Barnes suggests that Sumner was "probably the most inspiring and popular teacher that Yale University or American social science has produced." His skill as a teacher, Barnes thinks, made his practical influence on the mind of the nation greater than that of any other sociologist (*American Journal of Sociology*, XV [1919], 4).

12.   H. E. Starr, *William Graham Sumner* (New York, 1925), p. 2.

13.   *Ibid.*, p. 21.

14.   W. G. Sumner, *The Challenge of Facts and Other Essays* (New Haven, 1914), p. 5.

15.   Starr, *William Graham Sumner*, p. 31.

16.   See Henry Holt, *Garrulities of an Octogenarian Editor* (Boston, 1923), pp. 63–80.

17.   A. G. Keller and M. R. Davie, *Essays of William Graham Sumner*, 2 vols. (New Haven, 1934), II, 6.

18.   Starr, *William Graham Sumner*, p. 73.

19.   *Ibid.*, pp. 167–168.

20.   *Ibid.*, p. 543.

21.   Irving Babbitt, *Literature and the American College* (Boston, 1908), p. 88.

22.   W. G. Sumner, *War and Other Essays* (New Haven, 1911), p. 367. Cf. Van Wyck Brooks: "The classics had made spacious men and men prepared to meet great problems. . . They kept alive great

patterns of behavior, which all the American people had seen in action in the ample minds and characters of the earlier leaders. . . They appealed to the instinct of emulation, an instinct that in later days followed the patterns set by industrial leaders, by bankers and by millionaires whose only ideal was the will to power and who ruled by the blind force of money" (*New England: Indian Summer*, p. 106).

23. Sumner, *War and Other Essays*, p. 369.

24. W. G. Sumner, *The Forgotten Man and Other Essays* (New Haven, 1918), p. 11.

CHAPTER THREE. CAPITALISM, SUMNERISM, AND DEMOCRACY

1. W. G. Sumner, *Folkways* (Boston, 1906), p. 29.

2. W. G. Sumner, *Earth-Hunger and Other Essays* (New Haven, 1913), p. 70.

3. Sumner, *Folkways*, p. 18.

4. *Ibid.*, p. 24.

5. *Ibid.*, pp. 26, 195, 235.

6. Sumner, *War and Other Essays*, p. 150; cf. *Folkways*, pp. 30, 59.

7. Sumner, *Folkways*, p. 32.

8. *Ibid.*, p. 33.

9. *Ibid.*, pp. 58, 521, 533, 561.

10. *Ibid.*, pp. 99–100.

11. *Ibid.*

12. *Ibid.*, p. 100 (italics added).

13. *Ibid.*, p. 41.

14. Sumner, *Earth-Hunger*, p. 341.

15. Sumner, *War and Other Essays*, p. 186.

16. Sumner, *The Challenge of Facts*, p. 27.

17. Sumner, *Earth-Hunger*, pp. 359–360.

18. *Ibid.*, p. 345.

19. Sumner, *The Challenge of Facts*, p. 25.

20. Sumner, *Earth-Hunger*, pp. 351–352.

21. W. G. Sumner, *What Social Classes Owe to Each Other* (New York, 1920), p. 54. The argument of these passages is repeated over and over again in Sumner's essays. Cf. *The Challenge of Facts*, pp. 81–90; *Earth-Hunger*, p. 297.

22. Sumner, *Earth-Hunger*, p. 293.

23. *Ibid.*, pp. 228–232.

24. Sumner, *The Challenge of Facts*, p. 89.

25. Sumner, *Folkways*, p. 40.

26. *Ibid.*, p. 47.

27. Sumner, *The Forgotten Man*, pp. 465–495.

28. Sumner, *Folkways*, p. 652.

29. Sumner, *Earth-Hunger*, p. 294.

30. Sumner, *The Challenge of Facts*, pp. 89–90.

31. Sumner, *War and Other Essays*, pp. 175–176.

32. Sumner, *Earth-Hunger*, p. 215; also, *The Challenge of Facts*, p. 146: "How then is it possible to imagine that the human race will ever get its work done? If it ever stops to rest it will retrograde. It will then have its work to begin all over again. Poverty, if ever conquered and banished, will come again through the vices engendered in a world without poverty, and so the conflict with it must begin again."

33. Sumner, *The Challenge of Facts*, pp. 147–148.

34. Sumner, *Folkways*, pp. 5–6, 39.

35. Sumner, *Earth-Hunger*, p. 74.

36. "There is no hope of progress in politics save by growth, i.e. by movement which is guided from behind, which springs from antecedent facts, which advances by imperceptible stages, and which builds and unbuilds at the same time by infinitesimal degrees" (W. G. Sumner *Collected Essays in Political and Social Science* [New York, 1885], p. 102).

37. Sumner, *Earth-Hunger*, p. 238.

38. Sumner, *The Challenge of Facts*, p. 423.

39. *Ibid.*, pp. 201–204.

40. Sumner, *Folkways*, p. 118; cf. *Earth-Hunger*, p. 283.

41. Sumner, *The Challenge of Facts*, p. 419.

42. Sumner, *Earth-Hunger*, p. 285.

43. Sumner, *What Social Classes Owe to Each Other*, p. 9.

44. Sumner, *Folkways*, p. 64.

45. *Ibid.*

46. Sumner, *Earth-Hunger*, p. 41.

47. Sumner, *What Social Classes Owe to Each Other*, p. 26.

48. Sumner, *Earth-Hunger*, p. 42.

49. Sumner, *What Social Classes Owe to Each Other*, p. 37.

50. Sumner, *Folkways*, p. 169; *Earth-Hunger*, pp. 283–289.

51. Sumner, *War and Other Essays*, p. 204; *Earth-Hunger*, p. 289.

52. Sumner, *The Challenge of Facts*, pp. 261–262.

53. *Ibid.*

54. Sumner, *War and Other Essays*, p. 223.

55. Sumner, *The Challenge of Facts*, p. 340.

56. Sumner, *What Social Classes Owe to Each Other*, p. 120.

57. Sumner, *Earth-Hunger*, p. 300.

58. *Ibid.*, pp. 169–170.

59. Sumner, *Folkways*, p. 169.

60. Sumner, *What Social Classes Owe to Each Other*, pp. 110–111.

61. *Ibid.*, p. 98.

62. "In time the new men win their way. . . . Laws and institutions cannot prevent it" (Sumner, *Folkways*, p. 164).

63. *Ibid.*, p. 94.

64. *Ibid.*, p. 95.

65. Sumner, *War and Other Essays*, p. 164.

66. Sumner, *Earth-Hunger*, p. 89.

67. *Ibid.*, p. 119.

68. *Ibid.*, p. 131.

69. Sumner, *Earth-Hunger*, p. 83.

70. Sumner, *Folkways*, p. 29.

71. Sumner, *Earth-Hunger*, p. 139.

72. *Ibid.*, pp. 149–150.

73. *Ibid.*, p. 88.

74. Sumner, *The Challenge of Facts*, p. 44.

75. Sumner, *Folkways*, pp. 65–68.

76. Sumner, *What Social Classes Owe to Each Other*, p. 36; *The Challenge of Facts*, pp. 193–198; *Earth-Hunger*, pp. 126–127.

77. Sumner, *What Social Classes Owe to Each Other*, p. 163.

78. Sumner, *The Challenge of Facts*, pp. 238–239.

79. "It is impossible to know whence any definition or criterion of justice can be derived, if it is not deduced from this view of things; or if it is not the definition of justice that each shall enjoy the fruit of his own labor and self-denial, and of injustice that the idle and the industrious, the self-indulgent and the self-denying, shall share equally in the product" (*ibid.*, pp. 23–24).

80. Sumner, *What Social Classes Owe to Each Other*, p. 36.

81. Sumner, *The Challenge of Facts*, p. 25.

82. Sumner, *Earth-Hunger*, p. 175.

83. Sumner, *The Challenge of Facts*, pp. 44–45.

84. Sumner, *What Social Classes Owe to Each Other*, p. 36.

85. Herbert Croly, *The Promise of American Life* (New York, 1909), p. 10.

CHAPTER FOUR. CONSERVATISM AND CONSTITUTIONALISM: STEPHEN J. FIELD

1. 4 Wheaton 316 (1819).

2. Alexis de Tocqueville, *Democracy in America*, trans. Phillips Bradley, 2 vols. (New York, 1945), I, 274.

3. Brooks Adams, *The Theory of Social Revolutions* (New York, 1913), p. 215.

4. 94 U.S. 113 (1877).

5. 198 U.S. 45 (1905).

6. E. S. Corwin, "The Doctrine of Due Process of Law before the Civil War," 24 *Harvard Law Review* 366, 460.

7. *Ibid.*, pp. 371–372.

8. Dred Scott v. Sandford, 19 Howard 393 (1857).

9. M. R. Cohen, "A Critical Sketch of Legal Philosophy in America," in *Law: A Century of Progress, 1835–1935*, 3 vols. (New York, 1937), II, 266, 278.

10. In the Slaughter-House Cases, 16 Wallace 36 (1873), Mr. Justice Miller had rejected out-of-hand an interpretation of the due process clause which would grant substantive protection to property; in the next term he clearly implied acceptance of such a substantive gloss (Bartemeyer v. Iowa, 18 Wallace 129 [1874]). This suggests how rapidly judicial ideas were shifting in the 1870's.

11. 94 U.S. 113 (1877).

12. *Ibid.*, at p. 142.

13. 118 U.S. 394, 396 (1886).

14. 123 U.S. 623 (1887).

15. 134 U.S. 418 (1890).

16. In Allgeyer v. Louisiana, 165 U.S. 578, 589 (1897).

17. 198 U.S. 45 (1905).

18. Holden v. Hardy, 169 U.S. 366 (1898).

19. Tyson v. Banton, 273 U.S. 418, 446 (1927); Justice Holmes dissenting.

20. H. G. Wells, *The Future in America* (New York, 1906), p. 24.

21. The biographical material in the next few pages has been drawn from three sources: S. J. Field, *Personal Reminiscences of Early Days in California, with Other Sketches* (privately printed, n.d.); C. F. Black, ed., *Some Account of the Work of Stephen J. Field*, with an introductory sketch by J. N. Pomeroy (1895); C. B. Swisher, *Stephen J. Field* (Washington, 1930). These are cited individually only when direct quotations are used.

22. Roscoe Pound, *The Spirit of the Common Law* (Boston, 1921), p. 49.

23. Swisher, *Stephen J. Field*, p. 103.

24. *Ibid.*, pp. 16–20; R. H. Gabriel, *Course of American Democratic Thought*, pp. 223–224.

25. Mark Hopkins, *Lectures on Moral Science* (Boston, 1862).

26. James Wilson, *Works*, 3 vols. (Philadelphia, 1804) I, 126.

27. Lewis Mumford, *The Golden Day* (New York, 1926), p. 172.

28. Field, *Reminiscences*, pp. 85–88.

29. 9 Cal. 502, 518–529 (1858).

30. *Ibid.*, at p. 520.

31. 12 Wallace 457, 634–681 (1871).

32. *Education of Henry Adams*, p. 237.

33. Brooks, *New England: Indian Summer*, p. 97.

34. Quoted, *ibid.*, p. 94.

CHAPTER FIVE. JUDICIAL CONSERVATISM AND THE RIGHTS OF MAN

1. Butchers' Union Co. v. Crescent City Co., 111 U.S. 746, 756–757 (1884).
2. 4 Wallace 277 (1867).
3. *Ibid.*, at p. 321.
4. *Ibid.*, at p. 328.
5. 98 U.S. 124 (1879).
6. *Ibid.*, at p. 135.
7. 12 Wallace 457, 680–681 (1871).
8. *Lectures on the Elements of Political Economy* (1826), quoted in B. F. Wright, *American Interpretations of Natural Law*, pp. 308–309.
9. Pomeroy, in Black, ed., *Some Account of the Work of Stephen J. Field*, p. 51.
10. *Ex parte* Milligan, 4 Wallace 2 (1866).
11. Field, *Reminiscences*, p. 180.
12. Cummings v. Missouri, 4 Wallace 277 (1867); *Ex parte* Garland, 4 Wallace 333 (1867).
13. 4 Wallace 277, 321.
14. Beckwith v. Bean, 98 U.S. 124, 136 (1879).
15. 6 Wallace 318 (1868).
16. Field, *Reminiscences*, pp. 193–194.
17. 3 Sawyer 144 (Cal. 1874).
18. *Ibid.*, at p. 156.
19. Ho Ah Kow v. Nunan, 5 Sawyer 552 (Cal. 1879).
20. *In re* Quong Woo, 13 Fed. 229 (Cal. 1882).
21. 12 Wallace 457 (1871).
22. 8 Wallace 603 (1870).
23. 12 Wallace 457, 674.
24. *Ibid.*, at p. 670.
25. 16 Wallace 36 (1873).
26. *Ibid.*, at pp. 83–112.
27. Munn v. Illinois, 94 U.S. 113 (1877).
28. *Ibid.*, at pp. 136–154.
29. 100 U.S. 339 (1880).
30. *Ibid.*, at pp. 367–368.
31. *Ibid.*, at p. 361.
32. Swisher, *Stephen J. Field*, p. 285.
33. 100 U.S. 303 (1880).
34. 100 U.S. 313 (1880).
35. *Ibid.*, at p. 335.
36. 109 U.S. 3 (1883).
37. 110 U.S. 516 (1884).
38. 92 U.S. 90 (1876).

39. Swisher, *Stephen J. Field*, pp. 205–239.

40. 113 U.S. 27 (1885).

41. *Ibid.*, at p. 30.

42. Ho Ah Kow v. Nunan, 5 Sawyer 552 (Cal. 1879); *In re* Quong Woo, 13 Fed. 229 (Cal. 1882).

CHAPTER SIX. CONSERVATISM AND THE AMERICAN MIND: ANDREW CARNEGIE

1. George Santayana, *Character and Opinion in the United States* (New York, 1920), pp. 182–183.

2. *Ibid.*, pp. 190–191.

3. James Bryce, *The American Commonwealth*, 2 vols. (New York, 1895), II, chaps. 116, 119 *passim*.

4. Walt Whitman, *Democratic Vistas* (New York, 1927), pp. 308–309.

5. Dixon Wecter, *The Hero in America* (New York, 1941).

6. Bryce, *American Commonwealth*, II, 750.

7. B. J. Hendrick, *The Life of Andrew Carnegie*, two vols. (New York, 1932); J. K. Winkler, *Incredible Carnegie* (New York, 1931).

8. Hendrick, *Life of Carnegie*, I, 9.

9. Andrew Carnegie, *Autobiography of Andrew Carnegie*, ed. John C. Van Dyke (Boston, 1920), pp. 8–9.

10. *Ibid.*, p. 12.

11. Andrew Carnegie, *Triumphant Democracy* (New York, 1893), p. 20.

12. Quoted in Hendrick, *Life of Carnegie*, I, 37.

13. Carnegie, *Autobiography*, p. 367.

14. Bernard De Voto, ed., *Mark Twain in Eruption* (New York, 1940), p. 42.

15. Carnegie, *Autobiography*, p. 22.

16. Quoted by Hendrick, *Life of Carnegie*, II, 293.

17. *Ibid.*, I, 26.

18. Carnegie, *Autobiography*, p. 271.

19. *Ibid.*, p. 17.

20. Hendrick, *Life of Carnegie*, I, 49.

21. Quoted, *ibid.*, p. 73.

22. Carnegie, *Autobiography*, p. 87.

23. *Ibid.*, pp. 140–141.

24. Quoted by Hamilton Basso, *Mainstream* (New York, 1943), p. 89.

25. J. H. Bridge, *The History of the Carnegie Steel Company* (New York, 1903), p. 48.

26. See the statement of personal income, Hendrick, *Life of Carnegie*, I, 120.

27. Carnegie, *Autobiography*, p. 84.
28. Quoted in Hendrick, *Life of Carnegie*, I, 146–147.
29. *Ibid.*, p. 147.
30. Winkler, *Incredible Carnegie*, p. 3.
31. Bridge, *History of Carnegie Steel Company*, p. 113.
32. Quoted, *ibid.*, p. 195.
33. Quoted, *ibid.*, pp. 196–197.
34. *Ibid.*, p. 295.
35. *Ibid.*, p. 297.
36. *Ibid.*, pp. 188–190.
37. Andrew Carnegie, *The Gospel of Wealth* (New York, 1900), p. 129.
38. *Ibid.*, p. 132.
39. *Ibid.*, pp. 144–145.
40. Carnegie, "An Employer's View," *ibid.*, pp. 114–115.
41. Bridge, *History of Carnegie Steel Company*, p. 188.
42. Quoted, *ibid.*, p. 204.
43. Hendrick, *Life of Carnegie*, I, 399.
44. Carnegie, *Autobiography*, p. 231.
45. Bridge, *History of Carnegie Steel Company*, p. 231.
46. Quoted, *ibid.*, p. 233.
47. Quoted, *ibid.*
48. *Blackwood's Edinburgh Magazine*, CLII, 573 (October 1892).
49. Quoted by Winkler, *Incredible Carnegie*, p. 219.
50. Carnegie, *Triumphant Democracy*, p. v.
51. *Ibid.*, p. 248.
52. *Ibid.*, p. 273.
53. *Ibid.*, pp. 316–318.
54. *Ibid.*, p. 322.
55. *Ibid.*, p. 354.
56. *Ibid.*, p. 362. At the time Carnegie wrote these lines, or re-wrote them, the Republic was enjoying the McKinley tariff, now recognized as the high point of American protectionism, by which iron and steel had been granted greatly increased protection.
57. *Ibid.*, pp. 138–139.
58. Hendrick, *Life of Carnegie*, I, 274.
59. Carnegie, *Triumphant Democracy*, p. 155.
60. *Ibid.*, p. 216. This observation is particularly noteworthy as illustrating Carnegie's dogged determination to look at the bright side of American life. It seems nearly incredible that a man of some taste could point to the rifling of European art treasures by American millionaires as evidence of a domestic renascence.
61. *Ibid.*, p. 246.
62. *Ibid.*, p. 13.

63. *Ibid.*, dedicatory note.

64. *Ibid.*, pp. 420–421.

65. *Ibid.*, pp. 21, 320, 472.

66. "Where have monarchical institutions developed a community so delightful in itself, so intelligent, so free from crime or pauperism — a community in which the greatest good of the greatest number is so fully attained, and one so well calculated to foster the growth of self-respecting men — which is the end civilization seeks?" (*ibid.*, p. 106). "To every man is committed in some degree, as a sacred trust, the manhood of man. This he may not himself infringe or permit to be infringed by others" (*ibid.*, p. 107).

67. *Ibid.*, pp. 435–436.

68. *Ibid.*, p. 513.

69. Carnegie, *The Gospel of Wealth*, pp. 181, 123.

70. Andrew Carnegie, *Problems of Today* (New York, 1908), pp. 51–52.

71. *Ibid.*, pp. 92–93.

72. Carnegie, *The Gospel of Wealth*, p. 4.

73. Carnegie, *Problems of Today*, pp. 153–154.

74. *Ibid.*, p. 145.

75. Carnegie, *The Gospel of Wealth*, p. 6.

76. *Ibid.*

77. Carnegie, *Problems of Today*, p. 134.

78. Carnegie, *The Gospel of Wealth*, p. 4.

79. Carnegie, *Problems of Today*, p. 29.

80. *Ibid.*, pp. 179–180.

81. Andrew Carnegie, *The Empire of Business* (New York, 1902), p. 125.

82. Carnegie, *The Gospel of Wealth*, p. 102; *The Empire of Business*, p. 168.

83. Carnegie, *The Gospel of Wealth*, p. 17.

84. Carnegie, *Problems of Today*, p. 4.

85. Carnegie, *The Gospel of Wealth*, p. 18.

86. Carnegie, *The Empire of Business*, p. 136.

87. For a general statement of this viewpoint, see *The Gospel of Wealth*, pp. 1–44; *The Empire of Business*, pp. 125–150; *Problems of Today*, pp. 3–48.

88. Carnegie, *Problems of Today*, p. 18.

89. *Ibid.*, p. 29.

90. Carnegie, *The Gospel of Wealth*, pp. 11–12.

91. *Ibid.*, p. 19.

92. *Ibid.*, p. 22.

93. *Ibid.*, p. 15.

94. *Ibid.*, p. 18.

TABLE OF CASES

INDEX